GO AND TELL

A Case for Christian Mission Today

GO AND TELL

A Case for Christian Mission Today

by

VIVIENNE STACEY

CONCORDIA PRESS ▪ LONDON

*This book was set by Concordia on
its IBM Selectric Composer, in 10/12 pt.
Century type.*

Published by Concordia Press
(a division of Concordia Publishing House Ltd.)
and printed by C. Nicholls & Company Ltd.,
The Philips Park Press, Manchester

CONTENTS

THANKS

I am grateful to peoples of the East and the West, to my relatives, friends, colleagues, students, and other young people for their help, encouragement, and questions which have aided me in writing this book. I wish to thank authors and publishers who have given permission for me to quote their works. Also Wycliffe Bible Translators for the use of the hymn "Every Person in Every Nation" and Stainer & Bell Ltd. for "God of Concrete, God of Steel."

Vivienne Stacey

PREFACE

Miss Stacey has been a missionary for over 20 years in an area of the world dominated by a faith strongly resistant to Christianity. She has no illusions therefore about the task to which she is committed, and, as one would expect, the convictions, advice and strategic thinking expressed in this book have been nurtured in a very hostile environment. But there is no pessimism here, no suggestion that the missionary task is over or that it is hopeless. She draws great inspiration from the existence of the church worldwide as the fruit of missionary activity during the past two centuries and recognises among her fellow workers an increasing number of Asian missionaries.

She is deeply sensitive to the reasons that have led to much of the criticism of Western missionaries, but she does not let this influence her recognition of what they have accomplished. Now, however, she takes the stance that all thinking students of the history and the future of Christian missions must take — that missionaries from the East and the West are part of God's worldwide force for aggressive evangelism.

There must be a pooling of resources to meet the needs and take the opportunities quickly and penetratingly anywhere in the world. There must be an acknowledgment that short term and long term are not contrary concepts of missionary service but are to be judged only in the light of God's will for individuals and objectives. There must be the fullest use made of all the technological advances in the communication of ideas. There must above all be that flexibility and mobility which is completely surrendered to instant obedience to the Spirit's call.

I trust that the urgency and the realistic approach of this book will get through to Christians throughout the world.

E.W. Oliver
Secretary
Evangelical Missionary Alliance
London

Chapter One

SUCH MEN ARE DANGEROUS

Ability to mix with people, mix concrete, wade rivers, write articles, love one's neighbours, deliver babies, sit cross-legged, conduct meetings, drain swamps, digest questionable dishes, patch human weakness, suffer fools gladly, and burn midnight oil. Persons allergic to ants, babies, beggars, chop suey, indifference, itches, jungles, mildew, much poverty, sweat, and unmarried mothers had better think twice before applying.

This advertisement appeared in the "Church Gazette" of the Anglican Diocese of Polynesia. When in my position as principal of the United Bible Training Centre in Gujranwala, Pakistan, I asked four people to explain themselves, the written statement of each was in effect an answer to the advertisement. Without having seen it, they applied for the position advertised.

The first, Chaeok Chun, had just joined our international team at the United Bible Training Centre when she wrote:

I was born in South Korea in 1938 in a family which had a mixed background of Buddhism and Confucianism. There were no Christian visitors to the family as far as I can remember in my childhood, and I did not know anything about the Christian faith.

Two events in 1950 led me to seek after God. One was my father's death. Relatives and friends came to see him, mourning echoed in every corner of the house, and the incense smoke penetrated into everything and filled my heart with the mystery of death. I hoped he would either come back or become a good protecting spirit over the family. I believed that man's spirit is free from death and corruption, and I was taught that the body is evil and therefore corruptible.

In the same year the Korean war followed; it made me see and experience suffering. These two events controlled me with fear for some years and made me search for God at the same time.

During middle and high-school days I had been to Sunday schools but had no belief in God even as the Creator and the Sustainer of man and the universe. One day I was sitting on a sunny hill covered with wild flowers and said, "I wonder how all these came about." My friend, without any doubt, said, "God made them." It took me a long time to come to believe this, for I used to accept the evolution story.

At the Ewha University in Seoul there were compulsory chapel attendances and Christian studies. With the involvement in Scripture reading I began to take an active interest in the youth club and the choir at the Sung-Nam Church, but I did not know what it meant to be a Christian.

During the autumn term I responded to the Gospel which I had been listening to and by His grace accepted Jesus Christ as my Saviour, becoming the first Christian in my father's family. However I did not have any desire to testify to my conversion to the family or to my friends; it was a barren and fruitless Christian life, even though during the *college life I loved attending worship services and participating in the church activities. I did not know depth of fellowship with other Christians.*

Christ said, "Ye have not chosen Me, but I have chosen you." He did not leave me there but caused me to testify to what He had done by His grace, leading to a further step of obedience. In my final year there was a sense of deep awe, because the Lord's presence was so real and near to me.

At the Ewha Chapel, where over 3,000 students were sitting for the service led by Dr.Helen Kim, I sat in a terrible consciousness of the Lord's presence and listened to the message which I believed was from the Lord. It was about the people and the land of Pakistan. I was sure that the message was for me directly. Realising the growing urge within me to say yes to the challenge of missionary work, I began to read about the Islamic religion and country. On 5 November, 1961, two years and three months after that day, I arrived in Sindh.

It was there in the Sindh desert for the first three years that the Lord began to teach me deeper things of Himself and lead me to experience a depth of understanding of the bondage of sin in man and the world and freedom in Christ, also the need to participate in His sufferings for the sake of the Gospel.

Thus God called Chaeok Chun out of Buddhism and Confucianism to witness for Him. An Easterner, from South Korea, she became a missionary in another Eastern land — Pakistan, with another religious background — Islam. Chaeok Chun is now working with the Pakistan Fellowship of Evangelical Students.

The next account was written by one of my

students at my request. Esther was a Muslim convert, and this account of how she became a Christian was to be used as an Urdu tract in Pakistan. However, after it was written it seemed too dangerous to use it in this way.

A year later Esther was murdered — martyred. Her story was then published in booklet form — in English, Dutch, German, Japanese, Braille, etc. This is the account she wrote for me, translated from Urdu into English:

I was born into a respectable family in South India, one of a large family of brothers and sisters. By God's wonderful love I received the gift of salvation, and by His grace I have become an heir of eternal life. This is by His promise to me: "Whosoever believeth on the Son shall have eternal life." Thanks be unto God for His gift to me!

When I was about 17 years old, I was studying in the eighth class in a government school. Then, because of my father's illness, I had to leave school for a while. After some time I was sent to a mission school quite near my home.

Just as soon as I set my feet in this school, I noticed a Christian teacher who was different from anyone I had ever known. I saw her gentle way of speaking, her kindness to all the students, and her great faithfulness in her work. Her life made so deep an impression on me that I was really puzzled. "How could any human being be like that?" I wondered over and over again. Later I realized that it was all because God's Spirit was in her.

In this school I began to study the Bible. Two days in the week we studied the Old Testament, and two days the New Testament. One day in the week we did memory work, learning passages from the Bible and many songs. At first I did not study

12

with zeal, but rather indifferently. I had heard the Christians called blasphemers, and I did not like even to touch their Book.

One day we were studying the 53rd chapter of Isaiah, memorising some part of it, which was very hard for me. It was while studying this chapter that God by His grace showed me there was life and power in this Book. Then I began to realise that Jesus is alive forever. Through Isaiah 53, the first verse, He was saying to me with great sadness: "Who hath believed our report, and to whom is the arm of the Lord revealed?" Now I knew that I believed it and that His arm had been revealed to me. I knew that this was the true way.

Thus God put faith in my heart, and I believed on Jesus as my Saviour and Forgiver of my sins. Only He could save me from everlasting death. I only then began to realise how great a sinner I was, whereas before I thought that my good life could save me.

Now a living power began to work in me. When Satan would try to catch me with his nets and chains, I could resist him by reading the New Testament and trusting Christ. Sometimes Jesus would say to me, "Martha, Martha, you are troubled about many things, but Mary hath chosen the good part which shall not be taken away from her."

Now for Jesus' sake I had to leave my home and loved ones. He took me to Christian friends and gave me a home. After some time I was baptised. Then I could say with a full faith that Jesus is the Giver of salvation and peace. Such peace the world cannot give; it is the gift of God.

Esther's ambition was to be a missionary to her own people — a Pakistani convert from Islam telling her own people about the riches of Christ.

For a brief time she was just that — until someone killed her for it.

The third person, an Englishman, Milton Cashman, is a Christian business man whom God called to witness for Him in India and in Holland. Mr. Cashman told me that usually he writes only business memoranda, yet he wrote this account about his work in India:

"In all your ways acknowledge Him, and He will direct your paths," Proverbs 3:6.

This was the text of the address given to us at our wedding service in 1962, some months before we left for India. During the intervening years since then we have proved the truth of this text.

Our departure for India in December 1962 was neither the commencement nor culmination of any great master plan of mine, nor was it the result of inside information from the long-term weather forecasters regarding the English winter that was to follow. I had merely said yes when asked if I would consider going to India in a technical capacity on behalf of the company for which I work. The final decision to go was only taken after sincerely and prayerfully asking God to make straight our path. This involved the removal of various obstacles which seemed insurmountable at the time.

It meant withdrawing from many of the activities of our church in which we were involved and in particular youth work in the Pathfinder movement. We saw the answer to prayer as others came forward to undertake the work that we had been doing. We believed too that God had a purpose for us in India, and before long we were to find that just as my past scientific and industrial experience was invaluable in my new secular assignment, so too our experience as Bible class and youth leaders was to be used in the local church which we attended. My former connections with I.V.F. were also responsible for an invitation to help the activities of the Union of Evangelical Students.

Today, although it is possible to fly from London to Bombay in just over 10 hours, cultural and climatic adjustments for most West Europeans take considerably longer. We had benefited from a week's orientation course given by Overseas Service, aimed at encouraging a sense of responsible partnership amongst those going abroad.

We were helped to an even greater extent by the Bible and Medical Missionary Fellowship, which has extensive educational, medical, and evangelistic work in Western India. We were admitted to the fellowship as Field Partners. The designation of field partner does not confer on the recipient a form of junior missionary status but rather enables one to benefit from the friendship, encouragement, and prayer support of the mission.

India is as vast and complex as the problems confronting it, and because of this no two people react in the same way toward that great land with its population of 500 millions. For me, India with her democratic institutions and freedom of speech claimed my loyalty and my affections, I was fortunate in that my job enabled me to work toward the goal for which India's fast-growing industrial economy is striving, namely that of integration and the use of indigenous raw materials, with the ultimate object of reducing the drain on the country's foreign exchange reserves.

As a Christian in industry there were moments when one had to take a stand against corruption in one form or another. I believe that it is most important that the Christian, whatever his vocation, should be one who can be relied upon for an honest assessment and impartial judgment. Unfortunately, integrity in the world of industry and commerce is becoming a rare and precious commodity. This is just as true of Europe and America as it is of India.

A high percentage of the larger industries in India are founded with foreign collaboration. Foreign investment in India is now running at a high rate, and over 60% of the foreign capital invested in India is British. It is said that there are now more foreigners in India than there were prior to independence.

Only a very small percentage of the foreign population are Christians. This should be a challenge to Christian business men — engineers, scientists, lecturers, etc. India welcomes men who will work as partners in building up its economy. The church in India welcomes those who will participate in its life. Those who are prepared to go will find life more challenging as they share their skills and thus help to equip others better for the task before them.

Is it not preferable that the future leaders of Indian industry should acquire their technical and managerial skills through working with men of Christian convictions and integrity, rather than from a Western materialist? We found our life in India challenging and enjoyable and immensely worthwhile. I trust that some of you who read this will also find it so.

The last of the four is an Englishwoman. You may query, Why three women and only one man? Well, most missionaries are women. (Where are the men?) Anyway, let's hear from yet another woman, Hester Quirk.

It was too easy to get a post as physics teacher in the late 1940s. I started work in a most attractive part of the Yorkshire dales in a school with a long tradition of high standards and a most friendly and helpful atmosphere both in the staff room and the school at large. I was in at the deep end!

Two girls were taking Oxford and Cambridge entrance exams and other scholarships of various ilks. They had had a good grounding, and I got off on the right foot and enjoyed teaching immensely after the factory work which had been my lot for a year at the end of the war.

A Bible class occupied Sunday afternoons, and inter-school camps run by the Scripture Union took up a lot of the summer holidays, and through the few ensuing years I graduated from kitchen helper to caterer, to treasurer, adjutant, and finally commandant and inevitably emerged with some priceless memories, such as that of the awful stench as the kitchen team, armed with spades, buried a huge panful of stew that had "gone off" overnight and hoped that the police wouldn't feel led to investigate!

I also emerged thoroughly committed to the missionary cause; this came about through meeting a most intriguing woman who had come as nurse to the camps. She had been in India, and we were left in no doubt as to our privileged position here and our responsibility to the rest of the world. She had conviction and the courage to tell us that we ought to care, we ought to give, we ought to pray for Christ's "other sheep".

Having quite a sensitive conscience and really wanting to use my life for God, I enlisted as a prayer partner for the work in the Indian sub-

continent about which we had heard. It wasn't vague! A booklet was supplied which gave details of the schools, the hospitals, the children's home, and the pastoral work. There were photographs (some better, some worse) of the missionaries, and I had by now seen many coloured slides of India and Pakistan, so the thing had "flesh and blood", and I could pray intelligently, though I didn't know what I had let myself in for!

"21st Day. Pray for a science and maths teacher urgently needed in one of the high schools." So I prayed and then cycled to the high school where I taught science and maths, and the Lord showed me that I was to be the answer to my own prayer. I was to go! It was staggering. I didn't want to leave my comfortable flat, the friends who meant so much, nor the job I enjoyed, but I did want to do His will; so I went.

I can't tell you now how glad I am that I did go to that place where God had planned that I should be. There was a lot of heartache, of course — health problems, as always in the East, language learning — but that had its lighter moments and tremendous reward as one gradually understood others and communicated more easily — and of course the problems of living and witnessing in a Muslim land; but on the other side there was acceptance by another people, new friendships — not better than the old but much more varied and most enriching. There was challenging work to do and responsibilities that would have been impossible had it not been for the assurance that in the place of His choice "I can do all things through Christ, which strengtheneth me."

Fifteen years is a long time, and it was that long since I had set my face to the East when an equally *unexpected call came to return to the West, to live in London to be on the home staff instead of in "the field" — and again I didn't want to answer it! I came, of course. Again it is good to be in the place that God has appointed, once more with a little flat and opportunities to show hospitality to the wider circle of the Christian family as well as all the joy of being for some a link in the process that joins the need overseas to their own sense of commitment to God, who is calling them and guiding them.*

Do it yourself or do it with your friends:

Consider: Who is a missionary?
Consider: In what different ways was each of the four friends in this chapter a missionary?

Chapter Two

OTHER FAITHS

Chaeok was a Buddhist, Esther a Muslim, Milton and Hester nominal Christians. They all found new life in Christ and will therefore spend eternity together.

It is not a question of Buddhism versus Christianity or of a Muslim versus a Christian. It is a question of man meeting man or woman meeting woman, one person sharing with another what he has found. Our common humanity draws us more strongly together than our different faiths divide us.

We all like to be the bearers of good news. The Christian Gospel is "good news" for all. As people who have experienced the joy and peace of friendship with Jesus, we tell others about Him. We know there will be an echo in each heart, for all — whether Buddhist, Muslim, Hindu, or atheist — seek peace and satisfaction.

People may have various ideas about how to obtain this peace and satisfaction, but on the whole they listen attentively to the voice of authority, certainty, and experience, and those who are friends of Jesus generally speak of their friendship with Him in such a voice. I am not here going into the theory of the matter but merely say that as healed people we speak to those who are looking for healing, at the same time respecting the beliefs of others. We meet others as human beings rather than Muslims, Hindus, communists, etc.

We do not claim to be the only witnesses. We know that there are missionaries of other faiths and creeds. We disagree with their teaching, but we salute their dedication. The theme of the following letter is dedication. It was written by a communist party member in Mexico to his sweetheart, breaking off their engagement.

"We communists have a high casualty rate; we're the ones who get shot and hung and lynched and tarred and feathered, and jailed and slandered and ridiculed and fired from our jobs, and in every other way made as uncomfortable as possible. A certain percentage of us get killed or imprisoned.

"We live in virtual poverty. We turn back to the party every penny except what is absolutely necessary to keep us alive. We communists don't have time or the money for many movies or concerts or T-bone steaks or decent homes or new cars.

"We've been described as fanatics; we are fanatics! Our lives are dominated by one great overshadowing factor — the struggle for world communism. We communists have a philosophy of life which no amount of money could buy. We have a cause to fight for, a definite purpose in life.

"We subordinate our petty, personal selves into a great movement of humanity. And if our personal lives seem hard, or if our egos seem to suffer through subordination to the party, then we are adequately compensated by the thought that each of us in his small way is contributing to the newer, truer, and better mankind.

"There is one thing about which I am in dead

earnest, and that is the communist cause. It is my life, my business, my religion, my hobby, my sweetheart, my wife, my bread and meat. I work at it in the daytime and dream of it at night. Its hold on me grows rather than lessens as time goes by. Therefore I cannot carry on a friendship, a love affair, or even a conversation without relating to this thought which both drives and guides my life.

"I evaluate people, books, ideas, and actions according to how they affect the communist cause and by their attitude to it. I've already been in jail because of my ideas, and if necessary, I'm ready to go before a firing squad."

Communists are missionaries. They have a mission. Islam is also a missionary cause — it is a missionary religion. Like Buddhism, Christianity, and communism, it claims universality.

"The missionary spirit of Islam is no afterthought in its history; it interpenetrates the religion from its very commencement, and ... Muhammad the Prophet is the type of the missionary of Islam."[1]

The absence of any formal priesthood or professional clericalism in Islam places the responsibility firmly on each believer to be an agent for the spread of his faith.

"The commendable lay missionary outreach of merchant-missionaries was further augmented in time by wandering preacher-saints, pilgrims, and mystics who comprised the nearest approach to the professional missionary that traditional Islam produced."[2]

[1]T.W. Arnold, *The Preaching of Islam* (Luzac, London, 1935), III, 11.
[2]Warren W. Webster, "Islam as a Missionary Religion," *The Bulletin of the Henry Martyn Institute of Islamic Studies*, Vol.L11, No.3, Oct./Dec.1963, Jan./March 1964.

However, in this century Islam too has gone in for the professional. The Urdu daily, *Dawat* (Delhi) of 4 October, 1963, reports that there is great scope for Indian and Pakistani Ulama (Muslim religious teachers) in Africa, but only those who have the following qualifications can be successful:

1. Experience in the field of preaching Islam in its pure form.

2. Mastery of the English language.

3. Ability to deliver lectures on Islam and its revolutionary message in different societies.

4. Ability to make use of radio broadcasting techniques.

5. Ability to answer fully the critical questions asked by Christian missionaries and to hold public discussions with them.

6. Ability to start and run English monthly magazines, weekly and daily newspapers, in order to reach the educated class.

7. Ability to start and run schools and mosques and take care of the mosques as Imams and preachers.

8. Ability to publish books on Islamic subjects and distribute them.[3]

Islam is a missionary religion. It knows the kind of missionaries it needs. But all is not rosy, as the following extract from a summary on the propagation of Islam in South Africa illustrates:

"Islam has great scope for the propagation of its faith in that region. It can change the destiny of the whole continent. But unfortunately Muslims are indifferent to the present situation .... Wealthy Muslim brethren, who spend lots of money on

[3]Dr. Sam V. Bhajjan, "From the Urdu Press," *The Bultin of the Henry Martyn Institute of Islamic Studies,* Vol.LII, No.3, Oct./Dec.1963, Jan./March 1964, p.56.

worldly pomp and show, give little for Muslim missionary efforts. There is not to be found a single hospital or poor house in South Africa founded by Muslims."[4]

The 20th century is the century in which many strange sects mushroomed. One is Soka-Gakkai, "value-creating society," an offshoot of a comparatively aggressive sect of Buddhism. "Don't hold a funeral for me but just throw my remains in Tokyo Bay off Shinagawa if we fail to achieve 750,000 families in the next seven years," declared the second president of the Soka-Gakkai of Japan in 1951.

After the Second World War this group had only a few scattered believers. By 1965 it had about 13 million members. How is this possible?

"... largely because of its high-pressure, coercive proselytising ... but also because of its cell-method of propagating its teachings, in which all believers engage .... People are tackled in buses and trains, accosted with literature, bombarded at work, and pestered when sick, with the result that many capitulate as the best way to get peace ....

"The movement also stages tremendous public spectacles, as when they took the National Sports Stadium just after the Olympics in Tokyo for two successive days, putting on a pageant *par excellence* which would attract any young person. The fabulous new temple erected in the shadow of Mount Fuji attracts old and young alike and provides a concrete focal point for Soka-Gakkai's national aspirations."[5]

[4]Dr. Sam V. Bhajjan, "From the Urdu Press," *The Bulletin of the Henry Martyn Institute of Islamic Studies,* Vol.LIV, No.4, Oct./Dec. 1965, p.25.

[5]"Soka-Gakkai," *Japan News,* Vol. 60, No. 2, April 1965, p.20.

These various missionaries of various faiths are committed to their respective causes. We see the dedication of the communist and the commitment of the follower of Soka-Gakkai. We now need to question what is worthy of full commitment.

Is the communist, the Buddhist, the Muslim, or the Christian mistaken? We can appreciate dedication to a cause, but how can we be sure that the Christian cause, for example, is the only final and life-saving cause? How can we be sure that Chaeok, Esther, Milton, and Hester will spend eternity together in joy?

Do it yourself or do it with your friends:

Look up in your Bible:

John 17: 3
Acts 4:12
John 14: 6

Chapter Three

SECULAR OR PROFESSIONAL?

Career missionary? Short-termer? Operation mobilisation? Peace Corps? Voluntary Service Overseas? Free-lance? Third Secretary in the British Embassy? Travelling salesman for Ford? All are possible avenues for Christian witness and deserve careful consideration.

Nobody likes to sign on the dotted line for very long. "How can I commit myself for longer than two or three years in our uncertain world?" a serious candidate could well ask.

"Let's go and see what it's like. We can always sign on later for a longer period."

The main issues are two fold: career missionary or short-term missionary?; professional missionary or secular job witness?

Short-termers are missionaries who have gone into the field for two, three, four, or five years to work in a Christian hospital, school, or college, and in recent years there has been a remarkable increase in their number. Some have used their holidays or special leave to do a three-month stint and enable a career missionary to have a short leave. Jonah was a short-termer with a 40-day assignment at Nineveh.

The churches of Christ owe much to men and women who have given a few months or years of service in this way.

Some missions or sending bodies no longer have contracts with missionaries for more than 10 years at a time on the theory that all sides — national, church, mission, and individual missionary — need to re-assess the situation at least that often.

Operation Mobilisation works on a self-sacrificing basis in many lands, and students and other young people generally join for a year or two. In India it has performed a remarkable feat in printing and distributing millions of pieces of literature. Yet at times its members are not well-orientated and cause embarrassment and hindrance to the church in, say, an Islamic situation that requires much tact and understanding of the local conditions.

The Peace Corps have earned respect in their social and economic efforts by young volunteers in many countries. Voluntary Service Overseas members have made similar contributions. One sometimes questions whether governments and other authorities concerned have always made the wisest use of the abilities and training of these young people. Where authorities failed in this regard, volunteers have been frustrated.

A remarkable number of Peace Corps personnel and VSO's are Christians and have borne witness to their faith by their lives and, when permitted, by their words.

Other Christians have gone out to developing countries to work for business firms like Gammons, dam projects like the Mangla and Tarbela Dams in Pakistan, or their respective government services.

Afghanistan provides a striking example of witness through secular organisations. In the 1950s God called Christians to that land to business and trading concerns, embassies, the United Nations Organisation, the World Health Organisation and other spheres. These were men and women of vision and prayer, who saw themselves as the advance guard of Christian missions.

I had dinner in Paris in 1959 with a Christian couple who had worked and served in Kabul, capital of Afghanistan, longer than many other foreign Christians — 10 years. In 1954 a Christian Community Church was established there, and the foreign community was allowed by the government to call its own pastor. On 17 May, 1970, the first church built in recent centuries in Afghanistan was dedicated in Kabul as "a house of prayer for all nations." [Note: this church was bulldozed down by government order in 1973.]

The 1960s saw the entrance of Christian workers from many lands to serve in various capacities in government-sponsored schemes, such as the National Organisation for Ophthalmic Rehabilitation and the Medical Assistance Programme.

In Turkey the situation today is very like that of Afghanistan in the 1950s. There are opportunities for Christians in various spheres but not for missionaries — neither for long-termers nor short-termers. Men and women without missionary status but with missionary vision and prayer are needed.

Teachers qualified to teach English as a foreign language can usually obtain jobs. Students can take the one-year course at the University of Istanbul which is especially designed for foreigners learning Turkish. (No need for a missionary language school!) After passing this course one can apply to enter the faculty of Turkish literature or of Middle East history, or one could study Islamics.

Studies in any one of these realms would be an excellent foundation for future service in Turkey. The constitution of the country allows each individual freedom to spread his ideas by literature, word, and picture.

There are opportunities in other career fields. The U.S.A. withdrawal of some personnel from Turkey produces openings for foreign technicians from other lands. Specialist doctors may practise in the country if they obtain an invitation. Researchers in tropical diseases could be used.

Tourists may obtain visas for three months at a time, writers for a year at a time. The latter share the benefits of cheap travel along with students. Peace Corps and VSO workers are admitted but must engage in no religious propaganda in working hours.

Paul the tentmaker would no doubt have longed to seize the opportunity in Turkey today. An advance party (to join the enterprising few already there) is needed to take these opportunities now. The day may soon come when the country will be wide open for missionary work, but we have no justification for waiting until that day, no justification for not preparing for it now, for the coming of the Lord also draws near.

So it can be seen that the Christian who is engaged in secular rather than specifically church work is needed, but he or she must be a person of strong calling and deep faith, or he will succumb to the religious or social influence of the society in which he moves. VSO workers, Peace Corps volunteers, and Operation Mobilisation members are also needed. All these are a sort of commando—shock troops gaining a foothold in places sometimes remote and difficult, where no missionary is now permitted.

Having noted the important contribution of short-termers in educational, medical, social and other work of the church, I must express my deep concern over the decline in the proportion of career or long-term missionaries. One reason may be that some doubt whether it is Scriptural to commit oneself for very long. It is true that some who began as short-termers later sign up for 10 years or even on a career basis, but the ranks of career missionaries are too thin.

When the trumpet call is uncertain, who will come for battle? In some churches Christ's last command about going into every part of the world and telling the good news to all is not preached. In the 19 years that I have been a missionary to Pakistan I have never heard a Pakistani preach on the Great Commission and the Christian responsibility to take the Good News to others outside Pakistan. Yet I have heard a Muslim convert from Indonesia warn the Pakistani Christians that the church that does not export will die. One is encouraged by the keenness of Indian, Korean, and Philippine missionaries working in other lands of Asia and beyond.

However, the question arises: How faithful are the churches to which we belong in challenging people with Christ's commission? We who can read the Bible for ourselves, do we really think that our age is so different that it negates the idea of a career calling to missionary work? Where are the young people who, turned out of one mission country, will seek another?

We do not live in an age of opening and closing doors but in an age of revolving doors. We may be out of one land for 10 years and then back again.

It is the career missionary, the long-termer, who

has time to learn the language and study the customs, to become more thoroughly orientated. Life is not long enough to learn many languages, and orientation to one country can take years.

Without a corps of seasoned troops the work of short-termers would lack meaning, purpose, and depth. Where more seasoned troops (long-termers) are lacking, short-termers become fillers of gaps, holding the ground until much needed reinforcements arrive to stay.

Some who consider career missionary service are sensitive to the fact that the government of the land may not want them, that the church may be divided in its attitude to missionaries — some wanting them and some rejecting them. "The missionary vocation is a permanent invitation to misunderstanding," [1] writes Douglas Webster in his excellent book, *Yes to Mission*.

Primarily the missionary goes out because Christ and His church have sent him. In this age of developing nationalism and political uncertainty, being misunderstood is an occupational hazard.

Ezekiel was not sent to a people of foreign speech and difficult language, but he was warned that even though they understood the words, the people would not listen to the message. He carried on with his mission despite lack of success because God had commissioned and sent him.

Christian success can be measured only in terms of obedience and testimony. If evident results were the prime test, or indeed a valid test, Christian missions in some Muslim countries would have packed up long ago. God requires us to be obedient. Whether or not we are successful is His business.

[1]SCM Press, London 1966, p.26.

Some people are disillusioned with the organised church and want to dissociate themselves from it. This is unrealistic. The church, however imperfect, is in essence God's creation, and He pleases to use it. We need like John the Divine to see the churches — seven or more — after we have looked at the glorified Christ. Only then will we have the right perspective. Only then will we find our place in the mission and ministry.

Disobedience to Christ's command must be one reason for the depleted number and small proportion of career missionaries. Paul declared, on being called to missionary service for life: "I was not disobedient to the heavenly vision."

Some whom God has chosen to work abroad have decided to remain at home. For this they are accountable to God, but this disobedience results in incalculable loss to themselves and others. We, of course, are not necessary to God in evangelising His world, but if He pleases to call us to share in this ministry, it is incredible that we should refuse so holy and compelling a summons.

One state is not more holy or blessed than another, but all through history God has been calling men and women to witness for Him away from home, in other lands. No man takes this service on himself with impunity. We cannot be effective long-termers unless we are also willing to be short-termers. Conversely, we cannot be effective short-termers unless we are also willing to be long-termers. We can be acceptable professionals only if we are willing to be nonprofessionals, and vice versa. Everything depends on obedience, for God's demands are absolute.

Do it yourself or do it with your friends:

1. Should the number of non-Christians at home cause us to postpone missionary work abroad? Matthew 24:14; John 9:4; Acts 1:8; Romans 15:20-21.

2. What motives does Scripture suggest for engaging in missionary work? Acts 16:10, 17:16-17; Romans 1:14-16; 1 Corinthians 9:16; 2 Corinthians 5:14-15.

3. Is there any Biblical basis for believing that we are "saved to serve" and that God has a purpose for each individual Christian life? 2 Corinthians 5:18-20; 1 Peter 2:9; Ephesians 2:10; Romans 12:6-8.

4. How may we discover whether His plan for us lies at home or abroad? Ezra 8:21; Psalm 25:9-12; John 4:35; Acts 16:6-10, 22:10.

5. What would be the result of disobedience to His call? Ezekiel 33:8; Jonah; Hebrews 12:25.

Chapter Four

LET EVERYONE HEAR HIM!

"God is dead." I suppose He must be. He gave an order: "Go, and announce good news in every country to everybody," but so few ever take Him at His word.

You may find a missionary group in a Muslim land whose personnel stem from a dozen countries. Some of them stress the universal character of the church, and that is why they came. Others felt inclined to "social action," and their philosophy of mission brought them.

A few believe God is alive and took Him at His word, for if He did rise from the dead and is alive forever, His last words before returning to the eternal world should be taken seriously.

Why Christianity anyway? Why not Islam? Buddhism? Communism? Well, you might believe a bus is going to Hampstead from Reading, but if it's actually going to Land's End, you won't get to Hampstead.

Where is the final certainty? Is there an authentic and final voice? Did God speak in Christ? Is He the final Word of God?

The evidence is pretty good, but few will be convinced just because Christ lived a perfect life and claimed to reveal God. The final test is experience.

God does not allow us to try Him out. It's all or nothing. We take a step in the dark toward Him or we don't. He doesn't deal in half light.

A poet wrote: "Taste, and see that the Lord is good." A handicapped man said: "Once I was blind, but now I see," and it applied to his spirit too. Only if you fall in love can you really know what love is. You can read about it, analyse it, talk about it, but only experience really proves it to you.

Christianity claims that God is very much alive. It is we who are half dead. Christ rose from the grave. No one else has done that on a long-term basis.

Those who get in touch with God through Christ receive a new quality of life. It impels some of them to talk about their friendship with God, and they start reading the Bible as a sort of guidebook. It is a rather long guidebook, but then life can last rather a long time, and we need plenty of cautions, warnings, encouragements, and even commands.

Commands are not very popular these days, but if God gives them, shouldn't we sit up and take notice? Christ did say: "Go into all the world, and preach the Gospel to the whole creation" (Mark 16:15). Christians are taking a long time in obeying.

Once I was travelling through a remote part of a desert in the East. I saw a house and called on the women, who were in a section by themselves, because, as orthodox Muslims, they were allowed to see no men except their relatives.

They had just heard of the death of President Kennedy, which had occurred in the West a few days before. I asked if they had heard about the death of Jesus Christ on a cross. They hadn't. Nor did they know that He had risen from His grave.

Bad news had travelled fast — in a few days. Good news had travelled so slowly in nearly 2,000 years that it hadn't reached them until I arrived.

No one is going to dream up the good news about Jesus. It is based on facts, and facts have to be told. Whether or not the hearers grasp the significance of the facts is another matter, but until they hear them they haven't a chance.

One doesn't have to be a missionary to spread these facts. As it happens, I am, but with regard to the opportunity to witness I might just as well have been levelling sand dunes or promoting irrigation in that desert — a bit unusual for a woman, I suppose, but if a Christian man had been so occupied here, the men of the household would also have heard the good news.

Now God isn't selective. For Him there's no super race, no super colour, no super sex. He wants everyone to hear about Himself. It is quite something to take on everybody, but you'd expect God to do things in a big way.

Sir Henry Holland, who worked for over 50 years in the northwest frontier area of India (now Pakistan) had this motto on his mantlepiece when he was a college student: "Not for ours only." His friend thought he must be mad. What on earth did the motto mean?

"Don't you know?" said Henry. "Well, it means Christ didn't die for just me and my sins but for everyone's."

Not surprising that Sir Holland landed up on the northwest frontier.

Quite exciting too. He made himself into a good doctor, and the Pakistanis even decorated him. God made him an ambassador. "We are ambassadors for Christ."

I don't imagine that Sir Holland thought he had beautiful feet. Climbing around those mountains at Quetta or messing around after the earthquake, he would probably have had dirty feet and not beautiful ones in a literal sense. But think of the words of Isaiah, a spokesman for the Almighty, who wrote before the invention of printing: "How beautiful are the feet of those who preach good news!" (Quoted by Paul, alias Saul, in Romans 10:15)

We all know there's a population explosion on, and more people need to get their feet dirty like Sir Henry Holland, although they may not be knighted for it.

The trouble with this kind of campaign is that there is a hidden enemy like the Viet Cong. He's a sort of devil, who makes people blind to light and deaf to truth. His time is limited, but so is ours. God intends to wind up everything fairly soon, so we must get on with the job.

Not all Christians agree with these words of Martin Achard: "The evangelisation of the world is not a matter of words or activity but of presence, the presence of the people of God in the midst of humanity, the presence of God among His people,"[1] or of W.M. Horton: "It is a great mistake from the point of view of strategy to allow the straight preaching of the Gospel to bulk too largely."[2]

Against these ideas it can be argued that while in evangelism one needs to be present, not absent, words as well as deeds are called for.

The Student Volunteer Movement defined evan-

[1] As quoted by J. Oswald Sanders, "Singapore Outlook," *East Asia Millions*, October 1967, p.85.
[2] Ibid., p.85.

gelism as "the presentation of the Gospel in such a manner to every soul in the world that the responsibility for what is done with it shall no longer rest upon the Christian church or any individual Christian but shall rest upon each man's head for himself."[3]

[3]Ibid., p.86.

Do it yourself or do it with friends:

1. Is God's interest in people limited to any particular races or groups? 1 Timothy 2:4.

2. For whom did Christ die? 1 John 2:2.

3. How far do religions other than Christianity offer a solution to the problem of sin? Acts 4:12.

4. What is God's appointed method for the spread of the Gospel? Matthew 28:19-20; Mark 16:15; John 20:21; Acts 1:8; 2 Corinthians 5:19-20.

5. Why are preachers of the Gospel necessary? Romans 10:13-17.

6. Are the final victory of Christ and the evangelisation of the world a vain hope? Philippians 2:9-11.

Chapter Five

GLAMOUR, SACRIFICE, AND PIONEERING

Some think that glamour draws people to work abroad. I have never analysed the part that glamour plays in the missionary vocation, but after 19 years the thrill and excitement of working in a newly-created nation has not worn off for me.

My Christian vocation and vacations have taken me to a few of the most exciting places on earth. I recall a Boxing Day picnic in forbidden tribal territory on the northwest frontier of Pakistan, and a week in Oman in the southeast Arabian peninsula, where normally the tourist could not go, and a trek into one of the remote provinces of Afghanistan.

Granted that I have worked mostly in a small, dirty Punjabi town near Lahore, where in the summer we sweat it out at 110° in high humidity. Not very glamorous, but to our insignificant walled town came such celebrities as the Archbishop of Canterbury, the Moderator of the Church of Scotland, the Metropolitan of the Church of India, Pakistan, and Ceylon, and the American ambassador. A certain notorious American churchman comes regularly to help the cause of his latest schism. Exciting? Interesting at least.

In 1965 the residents of the centre in which I work — staff and students — had 24 hours to leave. The Pakistan Army took over for eight months —

just like that. Uncertain political conditions, a sudden war with India, elections — and one's life and work are suddenly changed. Forty-four pounds of luggage is all one may generally take with one, and only a few hours are allowed to select it.

Everything is a question of attitude. Some people may think that the uncertainty we experience is unbearable, but viewed in the right way it becomes exciting. Next week one may be working in another country and be out of that too after five years.

Which brings me to the subject of pioneers. The age of pioneers is not past. Who will be the first bishop on the moon?

Pioneering can take a long time. The Wycliffe Bible translators, thinking for the most part of languages spoken by rather remote tribes, say, "A thousand tongues to go!" Surely not a task that can be done overnight.

The Reformed Church of America has been pioneering in Muscat and the rest of Oman for 90 years. Thomas French, the Anglican Bishop of Lahore, was the first missionary to Muscat, and then Samuel Zwemer took over. Ever since the Reformed Church of America has been plodding on down the Persian-Arabian Gulf, and recently the Danish Missionary Society joined those workers.

When I visited Oman in 1969, it was a mediaeval kingdom. People used to carry lamps, not torches, in the capital at night, had to get royal permission to repair their houses, received guests from abroad only with the sultan's personal consent, and women were liable to a fine of 50 rupees a time for wearing dresses above the knees.

One day the 20th century shook this large

kingdom and its three quarters of a million Muslim inhabitants. During the summer of 1970 the present ruler deposed his father and inaugurated an era of reform and development. The country became open for pioneers of all sorts — road builders, town planners, Peace Corps workers, etc. Oil had been discovered in 1964, and oil resources are being developed and industry is being diversified.

What do you know of Trucial States, now called the United Arab Emirates — seven large estates on the east coast of Arabia, famous for piracy? Abu Dhabi has oil, as does Dubai, and in 10 years their economy has been revolutionised.

Christian pioneers are to be found there. In the state of Abu Dhabi I visited the Oasis Hospital, which serves one oasis and 10 villages, three of which are in the Kingdom of Muscat and what is now the sultanate of Oman, and I consider the men and women who work at the hospital to be pioneers. An oasis demands pioneers, and so does remoteness. You can't get farther than the cluster of 10 villages and the desert without a long drive over a new road or one of two weekly flights to Dubai. No other company; no weekend off; nothing in addition to dates and coffee, except what is flown in.

Recently the government of Nepal has renewed its agreement with the United Mission to Nepal for five years. A colleague writes:

"While we may no longer have mission projects as such in the field of agriculture, the government assures us of a very warm welcome for UMN agriculture workers who will co-operate and assist in the government's agricultural programmes. Changing circumstances and conditions are forcing upon us a new type of strategy, quite distinct from the traditional patterns of missionary activity. Hitherto the emphasis has been predominantly on mission-owned and mission-controlled projects.

"While opportunities of this nature may be coming to an end, a large door is opening to us in the form of multiple 'assistance programmes,' in which our personnel may serve in all types of situations in government hospitals, in Panchayat or municipal literacy programmes, in schools operated by local Nepali committees, in local hydro and technical projects, in state-owned colleges, and in secular programmes."[1]

Workers of the United Mission to Nepal have been operating in the country, and new types of pioneer activity are now opening up, as Mr. Lowe indicates. Kathmandu, the capital, has been a pioneer centre for reaching hippies and drug addicts who visit the country. Old-type pioneering also continues. Take, for example, my friend, who works at Pyersingh, two days' walk from Tansen, which is in turn three days' walk from goodness knows where.

When we talk of missions, we must not forget Roman Catholic missions. "Swiss canons regular of St. Maurice and of the Grand Saint Bernard established hospices in the most frequented passes (in Tibet); but between 1854 and 1940 11 missionaries paid with their lives for their attempts to enter the forbidden land. In 1949 Canon Tornay reached Lhasa. He was arrested and expelled, and finally assassinated by his guides on his return journey. Since then the Bamboo Curtain has fallen over the roof of the world."[2]

[1]Eric Lowe, reporting on the United Conference held in New Delhi, March 1970, in *Go*, No.1, 1970, p.10.

[2]Renē P. Millot, *Missions in the World Today* (Burns & Oates, London, 1961), p.114.

These Roman Catholic missionaries in Tibet were old-type pioneers. However, there are various sorts of pioneers: pioneers in the concrete jungles of the new cities and in the ghettoes, pioneers among the alcoholics and drug addicts, pioneers among the refugees. There are always new things to do; for example:

"The Holy See has nominated a vicar apostolic of East and North Asia for the Chinese of the diaspora; he is Mgr. van Melckebeke, the exiled bishop of Ningsia, now at the Schenmist Mission at Singapore. By organising an information office in conjunction with 118 priests in 52 countries and by publishing three periodicals in Chinese and arranging a correspondence course of instruction in religion, he has started a movement giving exiled Chinese effective spiritual and material help."[3]

There are many frontiers: frontiers of medicine, education, and social work, to name a few. Tomorrow has not yet been lived; it has frontiers and demands pioneers, even if they fly in jumbo jets to modern cities of South America. The missionary spirit is the pioneer spirit, for one never knows to what new endeavours God is calling His church and His servants. Christ was a pioneer, and "a disciple is not above his teacher, nor a servant above his master; it is enough for the disciple to be like his teacher, and the servant like his master." (Matthew 10:24)

You may work in an air-conditioned office in Singapore, but if you do not have the pioneering spirit, you will never be ready for new ventures of faith, and you will not share in the thrill of making Christ known in new ways. In one sense

[3]Ibid., p.122.

history does not repeat itself. Where the spirit of the pioneer is lacking, there is lack of vision, "and without vision the people perish."

People who will stick at it are needed. After all, the early pioneers were stickers. They did not give up easily or at all. Endurance, spiritual muscle, steadfastness are needed. Only vision will carry one through the drudgery, misunderstandings, and hardships.

"Christ for the joy that was set before Him endured the cross" (Hebrews 12:2 RSV). This is the verse which also describes Him as a pioneer.

Do it yourself or do it with your friends:

1. Name six modern pioneers working abroad and the kind of work they are doing.
2. Name some pioneers working in the United Kingdom and the kind of work they are doing.

Chapter Six

DROPOUTS, CASUALTIES, TENSIONS

In warfare there are always casualties. Some are temporary and others permanent. In the Fellowship with which I work in Pakistan our fatal casualty rate was about 8% during the 1960s: one teacher was murdered in her bungalow, and a young doctor was killed in a road accident. A few others faced health problems and were out of the picture for a while.

These were occupational hazards and must be reckoned with, for no one builds a tower without first estimating the cost. It is the less definable casualties that I wish to discuss in this chapter: squares and dropouts.

The 1960s have seen a marked increase in mental illness among missionaries. Some have come abroad fitted by their training to take their spiritual temperatures regularly. Others have studied how they might make a good social adjustment. When they have been somewhat unsuccessful, they have sometimes not had the spiritual and emotional resources to accept their failure and press on but have broken down.

Sometimes prolonged psychiatric treatment in a centre like Nur Manzil (House of Light) in Lucknow has provided the answer. In other instances the people concerned have left the foreign area of Christian service altogether.

It must be recognised that mental illness is on the increase in society in general, and so one might expect some reflection of this in candidates working abroad. Also,

"One of the factors about being a missionary today in any country, including the West, is the new forms of suffering to which he is exposed. Formerly, in the case of overseas missionaries, the sufferings and the danger were largely physical, especially arising from tropical diseases. Today there is much less physical risk, but there is great psychological and spiritual strain which makes up the cross for the missionary, especially the foreign missionary, whose foreignness adds to the weight of his cross."[1]

It is claimed that among career missionaries the number who do not return after their first five years of service is as high as 60%. After about 10 years couples who feel that they should take their children home for education account for further withdrawals. This occurs even when there are good facilities for schooling in the country of the parents' service.

Probably no other army in the world could function with such high losses. It seems to me that the answer to reducing these losses lies in a deeper understanding of Christian obedience and also greater care in selecting and training candidates.

The Roman Catholic Church is being compelled to debate the question of celibacy. The centuries-old tradition that those in holy orders should take vows of celibacy is being challenged. Some priests, monks and nuns are leaving their orders and marry-

[1]Webster, *Yes to Mission*, p.102.

ing. A minority want to marry and still continue their holy vocation. The pope is requiring that all renew their vows of celibacy. This has its effect on the mission areas too.

A vow of celibacy used to settle the question of marriage once and for all, and so the problems of Roman Catholic missions in this area of possible tension have been less. Protestants have recognised the contribution of both married and single missionaries and have welcomed the distinctive ministries of both.

The example of a truly Christian home is invaluable. Not all missionaries who are married give us an example of marital bliss. For some the adjustment to marriage, the demands of a new environment, and new work prove too severe. Grave tensions arise, and prolonged psychiatric treatment is needed for the couple. Such tensions react on the children, who sometimes show insecurity and instability. It is sad to observe an eight-year-old with good physical health but an illness of mind or spirit.

To marry or not to marry, whom to marry and whom not to marry — these are among the greatest decisions of life and can be solved satisfactorily only by the individual who is continually seeking the guidance of God, who has prepared for us good works that we should walk in them.

Many single missionaries in the loneliness of their places of work find themselves not as adjusted or as spiritual as they thought. A Roman Catholic missionary recruit has once and for all faced the question of celibacy and settled it, and this is peace, but the Protestant may have shelved the issue, never really facing the possibility of celibacy, or may have settled the question once — as he thought — only to find it presented again and again.

Christ spoke of those who did not marry for the sake of the kingdom of God, and to some God's call is, among other things, a call to celibacy, a lonely and long road, but in it is the satisfaction of being in God's will and being less involved in the things of this world. To avoid uncreative and unnecessary tension, it is important not to drift into the married state but to know God's active guiding in this respect. In knowing and accepting God's will lies His peace and the grace to overcome jealousy and discontent.

Christ's plan was to send His disciples at least in twos. Some missionary societies and church bodies locating missionaries have made the mistake of requiring single people to live alone instead of following the divine pattern of two or more working as a team. These mistakes have sometimes caused breakdowns and dropouts.

It is unquestionably a feature of the modern missionary movement that young or middle-aged couples leave foreign service (generally with the intention of returning, but they rarely do) in order to educate and spend more time with their children. It is no doubt God's will in some cases, but maybe not in all.

Some individuals trust God with their own lives but not with those of their children or parents. One of the reasons that made someone I know finally obedient to God's will to work abroad despite her mother's pleading was the thought that if she were disobedient, spiritual loss for her family would follow.

Missionaries coming from the West are probably too individualistic. God deals with us as individuals, but He also deals with us as families. Ezra writes of a riverside fast — not a picnic — that "we might humble ourselves before our God, to seek from Him a straight way for ourselves, our children, and all our goods." (Ezra 8:21)

The question of marriage or celibacy, children's education, the ability to "take it" are directly related to the Biblical doctrine of discipleship and to the concept of sacrifice. It would be cruel to say that all failure and uncreative tension are the result of divided loyalty or incomplete devotion. However, the primary qualification for any missionary is still and always will be his love for Christ, his obedience to Christ, and his knowledge of Christ.

We are in danger of being inhibited by theories of mission, traditions of the churches, cultural background, and plain human prejudice. We think we have rights, but as Christ's servants we have none. What we receive is sheer bonus. First of all we have to remember that we are God's missionaries, sent by the Father, Son, and Holy Spirit to do His work and fulfil His mission and plan.

John V. Taylor quotes these words from Bishop Lesslie Newbigin's study pamphlet on "The Relevance of the Trinitarian Doctrine for Today's Mission": "Faithfulness to the New Testament must bring us to give the Spirit a much more central place, not merely in the theory, but also in the practice of missions. He is still sovereign and free — free to do the unexpected thing that astonishes us, just as Peter and the elders at Jerusalem were astonished when His manifested presence was given to the uncircumcised Gentiles. He opens up ways that the missionary never expected, and when He does so, the missionary must follow.

"He chooses as His instruments people who

would never have been selected by the missionary. And when this happens, His decision must be honoured. He makes out of very humble and insignificant people powerful witnesses in the face of hostile powers that daunt the ablest and most resolute Christian strategy. He uses apparently small and casual deeds and words to shake the powers of this world ....

"When one has grown accustomed to looking for His presence, one discovers that precisely at the moment when all the human factors seem to be stacked against us, He bears His witness and shakes the powers of this world to their foundations. He does not depend for His victories upon the superior resources of 'Christendom.' He asks everything we have and uses what He will. If missions are indeed subject to the mission of the Spirit, then they need not fear."[2]

John Taylor comments on the foregoing. "It can be most misleading therefore to say, as has often been said, that God has left to human hands the task which Jesus began. Let us make no mistake about this. It is not the church that carries on the missionary enterprise. God, the triune God, the Father, the Son, and the Holy Spirit, remains till the last day the One who carries on this mission to the end of the earth."[3]

The mission then is God's, but what about the missionaries? They are followers of Jesus, who sometimes had nowhere to bed down for the night, who wasn't averse to washing other people's feet, who sometimes was silent when He could have answered. Now, there's nothing wrong in expecting

[2]*For All the World* (Hodder and Stoughton, London, 1966), pp. 24-25.
[3]Ibid, p. 26.

that you will sleep in the same bed for the next three months, but let's get it clear: we have no rights, no right to a bed, no right to sleep. If you start taking anything as your right, you immediately get away from Jesus and become a half-hearted disciple.

Some in the field may ask: "Why shouldn't a missionary have a refrigerator if the pastor in his home church has one, and it's much hotter here?" This is irrelevant. The question is: "What does Jesus think about my having a refrigerator?" It might be His will; it might not be. Let's make sure that our views on discipleship and sacrifice come from the Bible and not from people whose God is too small.

At least one theologian, John M. Allegro, formerly lecturer in the Old Testament at the University of Manchester, thinks Jesus was not a man but a hallucinogenic mushroom.[4] Who wants to follow a mushroom? Let those of us who know Him as the God-man take Him seriously. He denied Himself. He set Himself steadfastly to go to Jerusalem to die for us. The cross was central in His life and thinking, and it should be central for us.

Make Me Thy Fuel

> From prayer that asks that I may be
> Sheltered from winds that beat on Thee,
> From fearing when I should aspire,
> From faltering when I should climb higher,
> From silken self, O Captain, free
> Thy soldier who would follow Thee.

[4]*Time*, June 8, 1970, p.54.

From subtle love of softening things,
From easy choices, weakenings
(Not thus are spirits fortified,
Not this way went the Crucified),
From all that dims Thy Calvary,
O Lamb of God, deliver me.

Give me the love that leads the way,
The faith that nothing can dismay,
The hope no disappointments tire,
The passion that will burn like fire;
Let me not sink to be a clod:
Make me Thy fuel, Flame of God.

Amy Wilson Carmichael[5]

[5]*Toward Jerusalem* (SPCK, London, 1936), p.94.

Do it yourself or do it with your friends:

1.What are the arguments against single missionaries working alone? Luke 10:1; Acts 3:1, 8:14, 17:1.

2.If we believe God is calling us abroad, should the hardships and insecurity involved affect our response? Matthew 10:24-34; Acts 20:24; Philippians 3:8, 4:11-13.

3.What should be our attitude to opposition from our parents? Ephesians 6:1-3; Matthew 19:29, 10:37; Luke 9:59-62; Acts 5:29.

4.Does a feeling of inadequacy constitute a reason for withdrawing from service abroad? Jeremiah 1:6-8; Luke 5:8-10; 2 Corinthians 4:7; 1 Thessalonians 5:24.

5.What evidence is there in Scripture that God desires not only the salvation of the individual but also of the whole family? Joshua 24:15; Luke 19:9; Acts 16:31-34.

6.What is the primary qualification of the Christian missionary? Philippians 3:10; 2 Peter 3:18.

Chapter Seven

PEDESTALS AND MYTHS

Elisabeth Elliott, a martyr's wife, wrote her first novel about the conflict which is bound to arise in a missionary living a real life among real people. Her reviewer, Evangeline Paterson, says: "It is not a happy or a reassuring book, but it provokes the kind of heart- and mind-searching that we opt out of at our peril ....

"Genuine art demands remorseless commitment to truth, and one is given the impression that this is a price which the Christian novelist is seldom prepared to pay. Whether unconsciously, because reality is painful, or deliberately, because he feels conscience-bound to be propagandist rather than mere witness, he resorts to the idealised characters and inevitable happy endings which are the blight of Christian fiction."[1]

Elisabeth Elliott breaks through all this. She makes her missionary character a real person. She shatters the image. She is an iconoclast. She calls her novel *No Graven Image.*

Individuals have their own image of the missionary. Then there is the image held by the missionary society. Let us throw down all the images and look at reality. Biographies of the 19th century have sometimes emphasised the strong points and mini-

[1]"Her First Novel," *The Christian*, Oct.7, 1966, p.18.

mised the weaknesses of missionary saints, heroes, and leaders.

They were leaders, but were they saints? The public made them heroes. Perhaps they were leaders, saints, and heroes — all in one. Perhaps there were giants in the land in those days. But the average missionary is no hero and no saint. I am sure of this, for I know many, and I am one of them.

What about the pedestals? Some of my prayer supporters do not pray for me in the way I need, as they assume I have a greater degree of saintliness than I have actually acquired. Of course, if I write pious prayer letters with little sermons, I am encouraging this line of thought. If I never mention depression and discouragement, I cut myself off from ordinary mortals.

These lines are from an imaginary letter to a missionary:

"What does it matter if you topple off your pedestal? That way I can come to know you as a person and so pray for you with warmth and involvement.

"Isn't the heat unbearable at this time of year? How do you manage about clothes? Can you get books? What do you miss most? Do you feel isolated? What are the people really like? How do they dress? What do they believe? What's little Christopher doing now? Is there anyone for him to play with? Do you have to boil and filter every scrap of water? (If so, I ought to count my blessings every time I turn on a tap.) What do you eat? How do you cook? Have you made any funny mistakes with the language? What are the most striking differences between life there and at home?

"What do you find hardest to accept? What are your real problems?

"There is so much that I want to know in order to understand you and your work better, so please be (1) honest and (2) detailed. One difficulty, one incident, one day, one joy, one worry, described honestly and in detail are far more imaginatively stimulating than a catalogue of vague facts.

"I know I am asking a great deal because self-revelations, for the most of us, are a costly some-times painful, business. I am asking you to share something of yourself with me. Let me glimpse, through your letters, some of your ideals, your griefs, your encouragements, your cares, your day-to-day needs, so that I may bring imagination, sympathy, and understanding to my prayers for you, my dear missionary friend."[2]

Personally I want the images broken and the pedestals destroyed. I want to be accepted as a real person in my own country.

Then what about those ghastly missionary hymns? I've been through about a half dozen hymn books to study the words (not the tunes — that's another matter too): *Christian Praise*, *Golden Bells*, *Hymns of Faith*, *Youth Praise*, the *Anglican Hymn Book* (1965). Some mission-ary hymns have good theological content; one or two take note of urbanisation; most of the poetry and phraseology is 19th century.

The only one of these books I can recommend is *Youth Praise*, Book One (Falcon Books, London, first published 1966, 13th reprint 1972), a new collection of Christian hymns, songs, choruses, and

[2]Jean Watson, "Dear Missionary," *Crusade*, April 1967, p.19.

spirituals, compiled by the Reverend Michael A. Baughen, assisted by the Reverend Richard Bewes. It has a section on the mission of the church. The pieces are contemporary, and there are actually some new hymns: "Reigning Lord" and "Go forth and tell," written by J.E. Seddon in 1964, and "The fields are white," written by M.A. Baughen in the same year.

The Wycliffe Bible Translators wrote this chorus, and would that there were more like it:

> *Ev'ry person in ev'ry nation*
> *In each succeeding generation*
> *Has the right to hear the news*
> *That Christ can save.*
> *Crucified on Calv'ry's mountain,*
> *He opened wide a cleansing fountain,*
> *Conquered sin and death and hell,*
> *He rose up from the grave.*
> *Father, I am willing*
> *To dedicate to Thee*
> *Life and talent, time and money:*
> *Here am I, send me.*

I'm sure you know what I'm objecting to in the older hymns: the paternalism, the condescension, the images, the pedestals, and the out-of-dateness. Gandhi was offended by Bishop Heber's hymn, "From Greenland's Icy Mountains." Heber was Bishop of Calcutta and should have known better, but again, he was no perfect Christian; he made his mistakes.

Take the hymn:

Coming, coming, yes they are.
(Are they?)

> *From the wide and scorching desert,*
> *Afric's sons of colour deep.*

(Apartheid? Colour bar?)

> *From the fields and crowded cities,*
> *China gathers to His feet.*

(Really? Or was this pre-communism?)

> *From the steppes of Russia dreary,*
> *From Slavonia's scattered lands,*
> *They are yielding soul and spirit*
> *Into Jesus' loving hands.*

(Nineteenth-century geography and diction. Correct theology and out-dated sentimentality. Where do the communists fit in?)

India and China are described as lands of idols:

> *On China's shores I hear His praises*
> *From lips that once kissed idol stones.*

(Much more likely they are reading Mao's *Red Book.*)

> *Lands of the East, awake,*
> *Soon shall your sons be free;*
> *The sleep of ages break,*
> *And rise to liberty.*

(What about the new nations of the East ... freedom from imperialism, recent independence, economic domination. What does the Christian have in his song about today?)

Take Heber's hymn again:

> *From Greenland's icy mountains,*
> *From India's coral strand,*
> *Where Afric's sunny fountains*
> *Roll down their golden sand*
> *From many an ancient river,*

From many a palmy plain,
They call us to deliver
Their land from error's chain.

(Do they? How right are we, anyway? Is the West calling to the East, or the Christian to his brother?)

How should we educate our Sunday school children? What prejudices will they develop from singing:

See how in Africa's sunshine
Quickly "Black Brother" has heard,
And how the children of China
Eagerly wait for His Word;
Trustfully venture the children
From the far isles of the sea,
While the brown maiden of India
Lovingly rests on His knee.

One of the trials of home-leave is to participate publicly in meetings where such hymns are sung. How refreshing to join in the few hymns that relate to today and to 20th-century Christian attitudes, such as:

God of concrete, God of steel,
God of piston, and of wheel,
God of pylon and of steam,
God of girder and of beam,
God of atom, God of mine,
All the world of power is Thine.

Lord of cable, Lord of rail,
Lord of motorway and mail,
Lord of rocket, Lord of flight,
Lord of soaring satellite,
Lord of lightning's livid line,
All the world of speed is Thine.

God of Turk and God of Greek,
   God of every tongue they speak,
God of Arab, God of Jew,
   God of every racial hue,
God of Laos and Palestine,
   All the world of men is Thine.

Lord of science, Lord of art,
   Lord of map and graph and chart,
Lord of physics and research,
   Lord of Bible, faith, and church,
Lord of sequence and design,
   All the world of truth is Thine.

God whose glory fills the earth,
   Gave the universe its birth,
Loosed the Christ with Easter's might,
   Saves the world from evil's blight,
Claims mankind by grace divine,
   All the world of love is Thine.

                                    Richard G. Jones

We have departmentalised missions in our hymn
books and thinking. We have taken on the 19th-
century attitudes and sung them well into the
20th. We have set missionaries on pedestals and
projected our images. We have not faced reality
and so drifted into insincerity. If we describe God
in 19th-century terms, He becomes remote. If we
do not see things as they are, we may never see at
all.

Do it yourself or do it with your friends:

Write a missionary hymn.

Chapter Eight

ORIENTATION

There was only one properly orientated person. "And He was not at all like the psychologist's picture of the integrated, balanced, adjusted, happily married, employed, popular citizen. You can't really be very well 'adjusted' to your world if it says you 'have a devil' and ends by nailing you up naked to a stake of wood."[1]

Christ was fully orientated to God and men. He was always on the same wavelength as His Father, and He knew what His Father wanted and did it. He was not a college graduate, but He told His mother what He meant by being orientated: "Don't you know that I must work for My Father?"

We must accept the fact that the perfect Man must have been perfectly orientated. The outworking of His orientation was bad for His reputation. He was called a drunkard, He clashed with His family, He was thrown out of the town where He grew up, He was betrayed by one of His chosen friends. So today an orientated Christian may be called a "square," be misunderstood by his family, not keep up with the Joneses, be rejected by his "set".

[1]C.S. Lewis, *The Four Loves* (Collins, Sons & Co., London, 1960), p.53.

Christ's comments on orientation are equally surprising. He advocated no building society loan, for the Son of Man had no permanent home. He paid His taxes without grumbling or fiddling. He did not despise bank balances, but He challenged those who were too attached to money. He foresaw that the rich fool might have a coronary before he could enjoy his retirement. He knew the people who made covenanted gifts or had missionary boxes, and so He sent out His group with less than their 44 pounds of luggage, and they never went short.

His most unqualified statement on orientation to His gang was: "You are in the world but not of it." This raises questions not only for the Christian working abroad but for every Christian. How can one be in Oxford Street and not of it? Can one be a friend of drug addicts and homosexuals without sharing in the new morality?

When a Christian worker takes off and does 17 flying hours to the other side of the world, he is well supplied with instructions on how to orientate himself to his new environment. For a year or so he struggles to learn the language, customs, and thought patterns of the people. He is bound to fail somewhere, either because the standard is too high for a fallen man or because his definition of orientation is not correct. He can never sit where the nationals sit, because he might be evacuated in an emergency but they won't be.

What is orientation? It is turning your face to the East in order to find out where you are. It is a deliberate and prolonged attempt to know a country, its people, their beliefs, and language without turning your face away from God. Understanding others does not necessarily mean acceptance of their beliefs and way of life. It means referring everything to the vertical direction, that is, to God. There is no static definition of orientation, for it has to be worked out in a changing world in stress and conflict.

It is not only the Christian who seeks to be orientated to his society and his God. At every main bus station and railway station in Pakistan travellers see a notice with an arrow and one word upon it: *"qibla."* *Qibla* means direction, and the word reminds the Muslim to turn his face toward Mecca and say his prayers, even on the bus.

Christ too had a *qibla;* He set His face steadfastly to go to Jerusalem. The compelling motive for orientation for the Christian is Christ. He is the Christian's *qibla*. To be fully orientated to Him, to take up one's cross to follow Him is to start to answer the question, "What is orientation for me?"

Do it yourself or do it with your friends:

1. Make a list of the people you know personally from other lands.
2. In what ways are they different from you in customs, habits, and attitudes?
3. Outline what you know about a faith other than Christianity practised in the East.

Chapter Nine

RADIO, LITERATURE, AND TV

Population explosion calls for mass communication. How else will everyone hear the best news? Iron curtains, bamboo curtains, visa restrictions, refugee camps — how can one get through or in or out? By radio, by TV, and sometimes by the printed page. "The claim made by some secularisers that technology has produced a qualitatively new humanity misunderstands both man and technology."[1]

God is Lord of technology, even if sinful man misuses it. Redeemed man could use it rightly.

There are 14½ million radio sets in Japan with an average of five listeners to each set. So, 72½ million people out of a total population of 90 million listen to the radio. There is a TV set in every third home in Japan.

Soon there will be transistor TV sets, worn like wristwatches. At one end of Asia the Bedouin carries the transistor radio, and at the other end the factory hand will soon wear his TV.

Communists have plenty of hard common sense, and so they concentrate on literature and radio. Christians often lack sanctified imaginations and neglect radio and literature.

What about TV? It is the obvious way to reach

[1]Kenneth Cragg, *Christianity in World Perspective*, (Lutterworth Press, Guildford, Sy., 1968), p.188.

the most populous continent, where two thirds of the world live and where to be young is to be in the majority.

Oh, for a Christian TV station in Hong Kong or Singapore! Too expensive? It depends on what you think is important. Not enough technicians and specialists? Wouldn't you expect the God of technology to call Christian technicians and specialists in these days? He is always up-to-date; it is the church that lags behind.

TV is not visualised radio; radio is not photographed pulpit. Each is an art medium requiring its own study. Let's master these things! Obviously it must be a co-operative venture. What church or fellowship is rich enough or clever enough to do it alone? Anyway, why·do it alone? Will Christians get on with it now, or will they be 10 years behind the times and so miss the big opportunities?

Now, take radio. Radio evangelism requires technicians, electronic engineers, script writers, linguists, and others. The Far East Broadcasting Company has studios in many lands, broadcasting from Manila in 36 languages. The total programme hours of this station are the third highest in the world, first and second places being taken by Radio Moscow and Radio Peking.

The broadcasts of "The Voice of the Gospel" radio station, opened in Addis Ababa early in 1963, cover all Middle Eastern lands. At its opening one message of greeting included this sentence: "We pray for your creative imagination, Christ-centred dedication."

The pioneer missionary radio transmitter is HCJB, "Voice of the Andes." Today there are quite a number of Christian transmitters. That there are over 500 million radio receivers in the world is a significant fact.

There is the Trans-World Radio Monte Carlo, which transmits from a building constructed by Hitler for a Nazi radio network. Christian broadcasts are now reaching Russia, Western Europe, North Africa, and the Middle East on short-wave, medium-wave, and long-wave bands.

In 1961 permission was given to build the world's first super-power missionary radio station on the coral island of Bonaire, 60 miles off the coast of South America, and in 1964 TWR, Bonaire, began regular broadcasts. A former pirate base, Bonaire now has a large complex of studios, powerful transmitters, generators, and colossal antennae.

The equipment includes three huge transmitters. The AM standard broadcast unit of 500,000 watts and the two short-wave transmitters of 260,000 and 50,000 watts respectively give TWR, Bonaire, a combined transmitter power of over three quarters of a million watts, using 30 steel towers, the highest being 760 feet from the "antennae farm."

For the first time ever an entirely British-operated Gospel station has been built on the Seychelles Islands. This project is backed by the Far Eastern Broadcasting Association. The Seychelles are small islands in the Indian Ocean lying between Africa and India. From there good reception occurs in Pakistan, India, Afghanistan, the Persian-Arabian Gulf, and many other parts.

This is only the beginning. Space satellite programmes will one day beam TV and radio into every part of the globe. Worldwide instantaneous coverage is a near possibility. Let us wake up!

Radio stations accept advertising, and Bible correspondence courses have been advertised. Muslims who are sometimes embarrassed to talk to Christians can sit in the privacy of their homes and listen to the radio and take correspondence courses. It is interesting that thousands are enquiring and studying through these means.

A Muslim from Syria wrote: "I was looking for something on the short-wave when I came across your voice saying, 'Now is the accepted time; today is the day of salvation.' This was apparently the last sentence, for some music followed, and you gave your address. Truly that sentence bothered me very much, and it is still ringing in my ears. Can you please tell me what it means?"

The printed word can last longer and may be more effective than even radio and TV. The reader can refer back to print, and pass it on to others and discuss it. Millions of adults are learning to read — new literates. The clamour in developing countries is for more schools, more education of youth. What will they read? Whatever they can lay their hands on, probably. In Britain there is a good choice of reading matter and money to buy it. In many countries there is little money and little choice. Where is the flood of Christian literature?

Even 10 years ago more than 400,000 trained communist literature agents were at work in southern Asia and Africa. The works of Lenin, Marx, and other communist leaders then exceeded in circulation the worldwide sale of the Bible. Russia's expenditure on communist literature at that time was estimated at £500,000,000 a year for publications in 175 languages.

More Christian bookshops are needed, bookshops run by Christians selling Christian and secular books and magazines of high standards. More Christian books and magazines are essential. Journalists and translators, printers, business administrators, and salesmen are needed.

James Kayodi Boliria is the editor of the vernacular Christian magazine *Yorub Challenge* and co-editor of Africa's best-known English Christian magazine, *African Challenge*, which is read in many parts of Africa. The magazines aim to present the good news of Christ and lead readers to trust in Him to help churches by building up Christians in their faith. The magazines therefore deal with Christianity and today, with present problems and Biblical answers. One proof of the effectiveness of these magazines is the large correspondence received by the editor from readers.

The Bible is a best seller, but it needs new translators. Language is never static. Also, advances in Biblical scholarship relating to textual study especially should be considered. Historical research, development of linguistic and translational techniques — all call for new translations in the language of today and for this generation.

In the Middle East the Roman Catholic, Protestant, and Orthodox Churches have joined resources to work on the Common Arabic Bible, a new modern translation. The present Arabic Bible needs revision; in fact, a new translation is essential. For example, the Arabic word *dabbabat*, used for "creeping things" in Genesis, today means primarily military tanks. The Biblical use is now amusing.

Many old translations are very literal. Some of the older translators were afraid to depart very much from the syntax and phraseology of the Old Testament Hebrew and New Testament Greek. The

English Revised Standard Version (RSV), for example, unlike the New English Bible (NEB), is in the line of traditional, over-literal translations; e.g., Matthew 1:25: "And he (Joseph) called His name Jesus." "Called His name" is not English but a literal translation of the New Testament Greek, which here, as often, reproduces a Hebrew idiom. New translations are needed in the major languages.

And then, what of the hundreds of languages and dialects not yet reduced to writing? The Wycliffe Bible Translators often work in remote and difficult places in order to learn a language, and then print parts of the Bible in that language. Working for several years in this way so that a few thousand may read seems a long way round, but all peoples have a right to hear the Good News — and to read it.

"And this Good News of the Kingdom shall be preached to all the world" — by many means, including radio, TV, and literature — "and then shall the consummation come."

Do it yourself or do it with your friends:

1. Tune in on your radio to a Christian broadcast from abroad.
2. Tell a friend about the programme and how to get it.

Chapter Ten

ANY SKILL

Not drug distributors, not brewers, not hi-jackers, not bookies, not guerillas, not idol-makers, not kidnappers, not smugglers, but:

500 business managers
1,000 secretaries
500 accountants
5,000 church workers
500 dentists
2,000 student workers
5,000 teachers of various subjects
500 hospital maintenance men
500 technical lecturers
5,000 pastors
5,000 Bible teachers
5,000 ordained Protestants
200 chaplains
5,000 literature workers
5,000 industrial evangelists
5,000 doctors
5,000 nurses
500 agriculturists

800 radio script writers, programme directors,
and administrators

500 teachers of English as a second language

1,000 translators

500 radio engineers and recording technicians

500 TV experts

800 social workers

500 building supervisors

500 engineers

200 librarians

200 school matrons

500 hostel wardens

2,000 adult basic education workers

200 artists

500 booksellers

500 editors

500 writers

500 printers and publishers

100 pilots

Also ....

....

Please fill in ....

....

WANTED: All sorts and conditions of men and women — individuals skilled in all sorts of professions and trades and branches. For example:-

FOR MEDICAL WORK

Doctors

general, physicians
 and surgeons
anaesthesiologist
opthalmologist
urologist
obstetrician
 and gynaecologist

otorhinolaryngologist
psychiatrist
pediatrician
leprologist
pathologist

Nurses
general
pediatric
ophthalmic
orthopaedic

Administrators
purchasing agent
medical records
librarian
public relations officer

Other Areas

workers with the blind
medical technologists
occupational therapists
laboratory workers

physiotherapists
opticians
dieticians
X-ray technicians

Sixty thousand reinforcements! Only increased concern, prayer, giving, dedication could make it happen. The churches so linked by new personnel would be spiritually helped and come in closer contact with each other. We've never seen what adequate personnel could do; understaffing has been the general rule.

Whatever your job, there is a place for you abroad. "I'm a hairdresser," one girl told me.

"Fine! Think what you could do in the capital of Pakistan. Set up a modern salon, and you will be meeting half the diplomatic community from 40 lands."

If we have to be selective and if the personnel continue to be short, what should our priorities be? Leadership training is one priority.

Western countries used to send wheat and other staples to needy lands, but it became apparent that what they really needed was the know-how for improving their own wheat harvests — not cash but technical training of nationals. So with the church. If no one is evangelising, let foreigners evangelise; but, much better, strengthen the church, train leaders, so that they can reach their own nation.

As one Overseas Missionary Fellowship publication has it: "Today's alert missionary is more of a communicator than an activator. Between doing and teaching how to do lies the difference between building for now and building for now and the future, between strengthening the foreign organisation and building the church of Christ in the country."

"Theological education by extension" is a recent way of training more church leaders. This project originated at the Presbyterian Seminary in Guatemala, South America, in 1962 but has recently become a movement and is being tried in various parts of the world with considerable effect.

Dr. F. Ross Kinsler of Guatemala reports: "The Presbyterian Seminary of Guatemala held its annual graduation service on 1 November, 1969, at San Felipe. This was the eighth year of operation as a decentralised institution, making it the oldest 'extension seminary' among over 30 now operating in Latin America. A total of 161 students were enrolled, of whom 112 continued throughout the nine months, attending weekly classes at 12 regional centres. These students include many of the leaders — pastors, elders, church members, etc. — of the 80 churches that compose the 15,000-member National Presbyterian Church of Guatemala."

Ralph Winter, editor of *Theological Education by Extension*, writes in the introduction, Book III: "Even if the extension seminary were just an alternative educational technique, it would be worthy of serious interest. But for one curious reason it is far more than that; it allows an entirely new resource to be tapped for formal leadership; it allows the renewal, the building up of the church by means of an entirely new approach. It is not just a different way of hammering Hebrew into students' heads, it is a new way for the living church to allow its real leadership to lead. The real significance of extension is its ability to do a new thing in a new age."[1]

Let us listen again to Dr. F. Ross Kinsler: "The word extension itself indicates that our concern in this movement is to extend (stretch, expand, spread, adapt) the resources of theological education in order to reach the people who are the natural leaders of our churches. Most of these people are mature men and women, married with families, settled in their communities and professions. So we must extend our seminaries and institutes to where they live, i.e., to the whole area of our churches.

[1]William Carey Library, South Pasadena, Calif., 1969, p.390

"We have to adjust our schedules to fit theirs, our thinking to communicate within the varied subcultures which they represent, our teaching to match their different academic levels, our materials to carry a greater proportion of the cognitive input. We need to extend our concept of theological education to include, besides candidates for the ministry, lay workers, elders, youth leaders, ordained pastors, i.e., those who carry the primary responsibilities in our churches and congregations, especially in those areas where there is scarce hope in this generation or the next for an established, full-time, salaried ministry." [2]

Take a couple of students from Dr. Kinsler's Extension Seminary:

"Julio Paz, 38, ... holds a responsible position as accountant for INCAP, an international nutrition research organisation. His family, which includes seven children, is also outstanding in its contribution to the life of Central Church. Julio is an elder, organist, choir director, and director of Christian education. He has served in the past as a leader of the national youth organisation and treasurer of the Synod. Not only he but also his wife and two of his sons are students of the seminary this year."

"Augusto Marroquin, 19, is in his first year at the National University, studying engineering, and he works in a printing shop during the day. Converted just a few months ago, he feels called to the ministry and is able to carry two seminary courses as well as his other studies and work." [3]

How does the Extension Seminary function?

[2]"What is Extension?" *Theological News Monograph*, No.3, Oct. 1970, p.1.
[3]Ibid., p.3.

The seminary staff set up centres in various strategic places, wherever there are enough Christians wanting to study. One or more staff members visit the students in these centres each week. From time to time all the students from the different centres come to the main seminary for a few days of fellowship and study. Most of the student's study is done at home in his spare time, and he takes as many courses at a time as he can profitably manage. He may take two or three years or even 10 years to complete the course according to time available and his ability.

This whole method commends itself particularly when the expense of a residential seminary cannot be borne by the individual or the sending church. It encourages self-support and financial independence. Many churches in any case will not be able to support full-time, salaried pastors.

. This method also encourages mobility of outlook. Any Extension Seminary will have different types and levels of courses. It will frequently reconsider the relevance of the curriculum. It will attract the mature, those who are proving themselves in secular jobs.

It mobilises the laity — men and women — and teaches them not so much in a classroom situation but in a way more related to their life and the lives of their congregations and pupils. It breaks down the division between clergy and laity, between educated and uneducated. It could mobilise all who have leadership ability and qualities.

If the church has Spirit-filled, trained leaders in sufficient numbers and various walks of life, it will soon evangelise in depth. "You heard my teaching in the presence of many witnesses; put that teaching into the charge of men you can trust,

such men as will be competent to teach others."
(2 Timothy 2:2, NEB)

A few facts to consider in the light of population explosion:

1. Every year communists print three pieces of literature for every person in the world.

2. Asia has over two million students and South America over one million.

3. Every fourth person in the world is Chinese.

4. Only 10% of the inhabitants of the British Isles go to church regularly.

5. Pioneer translation work in over 1,000 languages is still required to meet the need of 5% of the world's population in West Africa, South America, New Guinea, and other areas.

6. Approximately 6,000 Protestant missionaries from the British Isles are serving abroad. With those from Europe and North America the total is 45,000 to 50,000.

7. One seventh of the population of the world is Muslim, but only one fiftieth of the church's work is among Muslims.

8. Half the population of India is under 25, and half the population of Latin America is under 21.

Do you know the new names? or the old names?

Malawi	Nyasaland
Thailand	Siam
Malaysia	comprising old Malaya, Singapore, Sarawak, and Sabah
Taiwan	Formosa
Ghana	Gold Coast
Tanzania	Tanganyika

Note: Vietnam, Cambodia, and Laos composed Indo-China until 1954.

Independence — when did these countries receive it?

Indonesia	1945
The Philippines	1946
Laos	1949
Libya	1952
Ghana	1957
Congo Republic	1960
Cameroun	1960
Malagasy Republic	1960
Nigeria	1960
Tanzania	1961
Algeria	1962
Uganda	1962
Jamaica	1962
Trinidad	1962

Do it yourself or do it with your friends:

QUIZ

1.There are Christian radio stations at:

> Monrovia, capital of Liberia
> Monte Carlo, Monaco
> Manila, The Philippines
> Quito, Ecuador
> Luxembourg

2.Tirana is the capital of: Equador; Albania

3.Phnom Penh is the capital of: Cambodia, Laos

4.There is a correspondence Bible school of the air in ....

5.There has been a mass movement from Islam into the Christian church in .... in the last decade.

6."Christianity has indeed proved to be a revolutionary social force. Today the biggest hospital in the country is a Christian one. The Ewha University is the largest women's college in the world. Missions were pioneers in nursing training, in the treatment of tuberculosis, and in the care of lepers. Yet from the first all these activities have been subservient to the main task of evangelism. The church has grown because of the spirit of witness, a great love for the Bible, and the emphasis on prayer" (*Missionary Opportunity Today* by Leslie Lyall, Inter-Varsity Fellowship, London, 1963, pp.51-52). About which Asian country was this written?

7.Which Muslim country has 400 Christian bookshops?

8.Which countries were these pioneers connected with: Henry Martyn; Adoniram Judson?

9.Amharic is the language of: Ethiopia; Chile.

Answers below.

INITIALS

Do you know what these initials stand for?

1.	E.M.A.	8.	C.L.C.
2.	W.C.C.	9.	B.F.B.S.
3.	O.M.F.	10.	S.U.
4.	B.M.M.F.	11.	I.F.E.S.
5.	E.U.S.A.	12.	F.E.B.C.
6.	C.M.S.	13.	N.E.B.
7.	M.M.S.	14.	I.A.M.

Answers on page 81.

Answers to QUIZ, page 79.

1. All except Luxembourg
2. Albania
3. Cambodia
4. The Philippines
5. Indonesia
6. Korea
7. Indonesia
8. India and Iran: Martyn; Burma: Judson
9. Ethiopia

1. Evangelical Missionary Alliance
2. World Council of Churches
3. Overseas Missionary Fellowship
4. Bible and Medical Missionary Fellowship
5. Evangelical Union of South America
6. Church Missionary Society
7. Methodist Missionary Society
8. Christian Literature Crusade
9. British and Foreign Bible Society
10. Scripture Union
11. International Fellowship of Evangelical Students
12. Far Eastern Broadcasting Company
13. New English Bible
14. International Afghan Mission

Chapter Eleven

THE PART MONEY PLAYS

Someone drops a new silver five pence into a collection bag after a missionary meeting, someone leaves a legacy, a cheque comes from the Inland Revenue in response to the mission's claim for refund of tax on covenanted subscriptions and gifts. How does all this add up to the annual budgeted income of a missionary society?

In most cases it doesn't. Devaluation, summer holidays, general lack of interest, postal strikes — these are all still affecting missions, and there is a possibility of larger and larger deficits.

Here are reports from three different missionary societies:

"Income during last summer was less than half of what was needed to maintain normal allowances to missionaries."

"The effects of Britain's economic situation and devaluation are still making themselves felt, and we have not received the necessary minimum to carry out our commitments."

"We thank God that it was possible to send full allowances for August but regret that we could only send two thirds allowances for September."

Allowances or salaries are only part of the needs. Missionaries need tools for the job: work grants for travel and maintenance of necessary equipment. Besides these recurring needs, capital or block grants are needed to help with building, to replace a much needed Landrover for a caravan hospital, or to buy equipment for a mobile clinic.

Then the missionary society needs income to run its home offices and to pay home staff, to put aside for pensions and health needs, and to enable missionaries to travel to their homeland and back.

Suddenly war breaks out in the land in which they work, or there is a famine and prices soar. A reserve fund is needed for emergencies of this sort.

If the full amount budgeted for the year does not come in, what happens? In societies which do not guarantee allowances or salaries there are cuts and hardships, because the allowances are already the minimum that a person can healthily live on.

One short-termer reports on the results of such shortages in relation to the work programme:

"For a year I lived in the same remote village as Mr. and Mrs. C. Mr. C.'s work was to travel the river for 70 miles around, visiting the churches and preaching in unevangelised villages. He has a motorboat given by a home church — just right for the work. But Mr. C. had to curtail his travelling work for want of petrol money (£25 per month for a full schedule, including maintenance and repairs). For some months he was unable to employ a Christian youth to help handle the engine (140 lbs.) and with other heavy work. Mrs. C. found the washing and cleaning took two hours a day of 'visitors' time — i.e., Christian help and teaching — when they couldn't pay a girl to do it (both kinds of help together: £20 per month)."[1]

[1]Anonymous article in "The Overseas Scene," *Christian Graduate*, March 1970, p.14.

Lack of such help for experienced workers is a waste of their talent, training, and opportunities in the midst of so many unevangelised people. The help is comparatively cheap, provides work for the needy, and enables the missionaries to be more effective in spreading good news.

Sometimes a balance in the missionary's account can be of help in evangelism. Once a missionary met a Muslim girl stranded at the customs in the girl's own country. The officials would not let her board the plane for the U.K. unless she paid £20 for excess baggage. She had only £5. After a discussion with the officials and the conclusion that no one would pay £10 for mangoes, the total was reduced to £10, and the missionary lent the girl this amount.

What if the missionary because of reduced allowances had had no bank account, no money to find this way into a Muslim heart and home? Incidentally this perfect stranger repaid the loan in due time, and there was an entrance for the Gospel.

If money does not come into the coffers of a missionary society, the planners find it difficult to undertake new projects, to launch out and grasp new opportunities. Societies vary with their arrangements about money. Denominational societies and some other bodies give a guaranteed salary to the missionary, and any cuts in the expenditure do not affect the salary sheet but do affect the work grant or the new projects' or the block grants for building or the taking on of new recruits. Other missionary societies share out what comes in, and so sometimes allowances or salaries are cut.

Why the decrease in giving to missions? We are told that there is a declining interest in the work of the church abroad. Listen to a church member from the U.K.: "Well, you see I can't give as much as I used to to missions, because our church is now doing more for drug addicts in Liverpool. After all, charity begins at home. And then there are those terrible pictures put out by Oxfam of starving children. We really must help Christian Aid and the Churches' Action for World Development and those earthquake victims."

It is perfectly legitimate and indeed our Christian responsibility to help in social concerns at home and abroad, but not by letting missions suffer. When all is said and done, this church member belonged to an affluent society. Many things considered necessary are really luxuries, and we could all be less self-indulgent or not self-indulgent at all.

Why should we give when we feel like it? Should we not coolly work out our commitments and then constantly revise them in the light of Christ's total giving? "Though He was rich, yet for your sakes He became poor, so that by His poverty you might become rich" (2 Corinthians 8:9). Not that just you become spiritually rich but also that African college student and the illiterate village girl in Indonesia and the farm boy in Brazil.

Money has its dangers, of course. In some areas the church is making tremendous advances through new programmes, especially in South America. In other parts it relies heavily on its institutional work. Resources are necessary, but the church should not rely on these for its spiritual power. Douglas Webster reminds us: "The church has to learn that its supreme asset does not lie in its material possessions and its own resources but in its Lord." [2]

[2] *Yes to Mission*, p.42.

In some countries schisms have been aided and abetted by money from sympathisers abroad. I think of a schism in an Asian denomination which purports to be about doctrine but is really about power. Who should control the institutions? Who should control the money from abroad? It is always wise for donors to have a good idea as to how their money is being used, and in the end the facts will out.

Sometimes the church which engages missionaries in its programmes regards them as cheap labour. If they put a local man into Mr. Jones' place, they will have to pay him! However, if Mr. Jones feels he is being used as cheap labour, he will apply for a transfer. A missionary principal once asked if a certain missionary society had an accountant and/or librarian who could join his staff. When asked why he didn't look for a national, he replied that he would have to pay a national from their already tight budget.

Another problem that money causes is that sometimes a missionary has a standard of living higher than that of the average man in the country he serves, and misunderstanding follows. The village school teacher may live on £20 a month and the missionary, also a teacher by profession, on £40 a month. What the national does not realise perhaps is that in his own country the missionary might earn £30 a week and that he has expenses for postage and the education of his children, expenses that are not so demanding for the national.

The missionary cannot always be like the national, and anyway nationals live at different levels. Someone once said to a missionary: "Why don't you live like the Indians?" The reply was: "Like which Indian?"

Money can cause problems among missionaries too. There are tests for those missionaries engaged in the same task but coming from different countries of East and West and all receiving different allowances. One might receive seven times more than another, and all receive more than their national colleagues. God gives grace in these situations, but maybe there are practical ways of sharing and helping one another.

This problem is not peculiar to missionaries. One Pakistani evangelist once said: "I am working for the Anglicans, and they pay less than the Presbyterians. Can you help me to be transferred or to get an increase?" The missionary explained that there are always inequalities.

Life often seems unfair. Godliness with contentment is great gain. St. Paul had to learn to be content in any condition. He was not naturally content, presumably.

This brings us back to the new silver five pence in the collection bag, to the legacy, and the covenanted gift. It is wrong to expect greater sacrifices of one's representatives abroad than one demands of oneself. To deny that they are our representatives is to deny that the body of Christ is one body.

"To whom much is given, much is required." We cannot deny that to us much has been given: a Christian heritage, an affluent society, God's unspeakable gift, Jesus Christ.

Do it yourself or do it with your friends:

1. How is missionary work to be financed? 1 Corinthians 9:1-14; 2 Corinthians 8:1-5; Galatians 6:6; Philippians 4:15-19; 3 John 5-8.

2. Why cannot one serve God and mammon? Matthew 6:24-33.

3. Why is the love of money the root of all evil? What should be our attitude to money? 1 Timothy 6:17-19; Hebrews 13:5; Matthew 6:19-21.

4. Why are missions likely to be short of funds? 2 Timothy 3:1-2; Titus 1:7,11

5. What percentage did the Old Testament advocate for giving to God? Genesis 28:22. What about us? 1 Corinthians 16:1-2. What percentage did Christ give? 2 Corinthians 8:9.

6. What should be our attitude to the stewardship of money, time, talent, etc.? Romans 12:1-2.

Chapter Twelve

THE VIEW FROM THE OTHER SIDE

Karl Marx considered Christianity a sort of drug addiction, an opiate to keep people quiet. Saul of Tarsus thought it worthwhile to devote considerable energy to the persecution of Christ's followers. Tacitus in his description of the trial of Pomponia Graecina in A.D.57 (*Annales,* xiii,32) says she was accused of "foreign superstition." This "foreign superstition" was most probably Christianity. Suetonius refers to the Christians as "a set of men adhering to a novel and mischievous superstition."

About two and a half centuries later the Christian historian Eusebius wrote about the persecution under Diocletian: "Imperial edicts were published everywhere ordering that the churches be razed to the ground, that the Scriptures be destroyed by fire, that those holding office be deposed, and they of the household be deprived of freedom if they persisted in the profession of Christianity. This was the first edict against us. But not long after other decrees were issued, which enjoined that the rulers of the churches in every place be first imprisoned, and thereafter every means be used to compel them to sacrifice."

Religious toleration was pleaded for early in the Christian era. In the Edict of Milan, A.D.313, Emperors Constantine and Licinius decided that "it was right that Christians and all others should have freedom to follow the kind of religion they favoured."

Julian the Apostate in his letter to the people of Bostra in A.D.362 wrote: "Men should be taught and won over by reason, not by blows, insults, and corporal punishments. I therefore most earnestly admonish the adherents of the true religion not to injure or insult the Galilaeans in any way, either by physical attack or by reproaches. Those who are in the wrong in matters of supreme importance are objects of pity rather than hate."

As in the early centuries, so now — persecutions and pleas for toleration. Certainly there is persecution today, although it is sometimes very difficult to know the true facts, especially about communist regimes. Richard Wurmbrand gives his account of the suffering and testimony of the underground church in countries behind the Iron Curtain. He writes:

"Those Christian leaders in the West who show friendship to the communists justify it by the teaching of Jesus that we must love even our enemies. But never did Jesus teach that we must love *only* our enemies, forgetting our brethren. They show their love by wining and dining those whose hands are full of the blood of Christians, not by giving them the good news of Christ. But those oppressed by the communists are forgotten. They are not loved." [1]

Writers around the world protested when two communist writers, Sinaivski and Daniel, were sentenced by their own comrades to prison terms. But not even churches protest when Christians are

[1] *Tortured for Christ* (Hodder and Stoughton, London, 1967), pp.64-65.

put in prison for their faith.

Of the church Wurmbrand writes: "Tens of thousands of such 'outward nonbelievers' exist in every communist land. They feel it wiser not to attend the show-churches where they will be noticed and hear only a watered-down Gospel. Instead, they stay in the positions of authority and responsibility they occupy, and from there quickly and effectively witness for Christ."[2]

"There is no clear partition-wall by which you could say where the underground church, which is the main stronghold of Christianity, ends and the official church begins. They are *interwoven*. Many pastors of the show-churches carry on a secret parallel ministry going far beyond the limitations put on them by the communists."[3]

In most communist countries the Bible is a rejected or branded book, hence the need to smuggle it. Smuggling anything raises ethical and moral questions. Brother Andrew, who has smuggled thousands of Bibles into communist countries, is known as God's smuggler.

"Lord, in my luggage I have Scriptures that I want to take to Your children across the border. When You were on earth, You made blind eyes see. Now, I pray, make seeing eyes blind .... Do not let the guards see those things You don't want them to see."[4]

"You were told to come eastward for 2,000 miles to get a Bible, and we were told to go westward 2,000 miles carrying Bibles to churches in

[2]Ibid., p.83.
[3]Ibid., p.85.
[4]*God's Smuggler* (Hodder and Stoughton, London, 1968), p.101.

Russia. And here we are tonight, recognising each other the instant we meet!"[5]

Only in China and Albania is there no demand for Bibles, for most of the inhabitants do not know what it is. The Bible is neither rejected nor coveted, just ignored. In all other communist lands there are great demands for this proscribed book. As tourists travel, so may Bibles.

We must listen to those who honour the Bible but who speak out against those who try to follow its teaching. K.M. Panikkar reminds us of the alliance of missions and imperialists when he writes of Christian missions in China:

"In the treaties that were concluded with the Powers in 1858, the missionaries obtained the privilege of travelling freely all over China, together with a guarantee of toleration of Christianity and protection to Chinese Christians in the profession of their faith. Thus was Christianity not only identified with Europe but reduced to the position of a diplomatic interest of Western powers in their aggression against China. The missionaries were clothed with extra-terratoriality and given the right to appeal to their consuls and ministers in the 'religious' interests of Chinese Christians. No greater disservice, as history was to show, could have been rendered by its proclaimed champions to the cause of the church of Christ.

"It is also significant that out of the unconscionable indemnities exacted from China after the various wars, the churches received a considerable portion. The missions thus started by benefiting from the humiliations of China and by being

[5]Ibid., p.196.

identified in the eyes of the Chinese with aggression against their country ....

"The treaty clauses, in fact, wrote the ultimate doom of Christian activities in China. To have believed that a religion which grew up under the protection of foreign powers, especially under humiliating conditions following defeat, could be tolerated when the nation received its authority showed extreme short-sightedness. The fact is that the missionaries, like the Europeans, felt convinced in the 19th century that their political supremacy was permanent, and they never imagined that China would regain a position when the history of the past might be brought up against them and their converts."[6]

Panikker analyses the reasons for this very meagre success of Christian missions in Asia, first mentioning the missionary's attitude of moral superiority and belief in his own exclusive righteousness. Hindus and Buddhists regard as alien the claim of any sect that it alone possesses the truth.

The association of Christian missionary work with aggressive imperialism, the second reason given by Panikker, has already been mentioned.

Third, the sense of European superiority unconsciously communicated produced its own reaction. "... no Asian people accepted the cultural superiority of the West. The educational activities of the missionaries stressing the glories of European culture only led to the identification of the work with Western cultural aggression.

"Fourthly, the wide variety of Christian sects, each proclaiming the errors of the others, handicapped missionary work. Finally the growth of

[6]*Asia and Western Dominance* (Allen & Unwin, London, 1959), p.291.

unbelief in Europe in the 19th century and the crisis in European civilisation, following the Great War of 1914-1918, and the October Revolution broke whatever spell the different sects of Christianity had among certain classes of Asians. With the disappearance of European dominance Christianity assumed its natural position as one of the religions of Asia, and the missionaries ceased to have any special or privileged position."[7]

Perhaps this influence of unbelief and secularisation needs to be stressed now. Kenneth Cragg writes: "With this technocratic human mastery goes the whole profound revolution we know, loosely, as secularisation, as a new quality of disbelief in the Divine and the sacred — new in the sense that, unlike earlier and wistful atheisms, it seems disinterested in its own persuasion. In Nietzsche's words it assumes that 'all the gods are dead, and man must be mature enough to go on from there,' while attitudes of mind and institutions of society are more and more shaped and determined, not by our independent beliefs, but by the pressures and demands of the techniques of production and mechanisation which we have devised."[8]

The great Indian leader, Mahatma Gandhi, had much to say about Christianity. Anand T. Hingorani edited and published his comments on the subject in a book titled *The Message of Jesus Christ*. Gandhi describes how upset he was by some street preaching he heard while a schoolboy:

"Though the preaching took place over 40 years ago, the painful memory of it is still vivid before me. What I have heard and read since has

[7]Ibid., p.297.
[8]*Christianity in World Perspective*, p.171.

but confirmed that first impression, I have read several missionary publications, and they are able to see only the dark side and paint it darker still .... (quoted from *Young India*, March 4, 1926).

"You, the missionaries, come to India thinking that you come to a land of heathens, of idolators, of men who do not know God. One of the greatest of Christian divines, Bishop Heber, wrote the two lines which have always left a sting with me: 'Where every prospect pleases, And only man is vile.' I wish he had not written them. My own experience, in my travels throughout India, has been to the contrary. I have gone from one end of the country to the other, without any prejudice, in a relentless search after Truth, and I am not able to say that here in this fair land, watered by the great Ganges, the Brahmaputra and the Jumna, man is vile. He is not vile. He is as much a seeker after Truth as you and I are, possibly more so ....

"Vile as some of them (untouchables) may be, there are noblest specimens of humanity in their midst .... There are non-*Brahmins*, there are *Brahmins* who are as fine specimens of humanity as you will find in any place on the earth ....

"You are here to find out the distress of the people of India and remove it. But I hope you are here also in a receptive mood, and that if India has anything to give, you will not stop your ears, you will not close your eyes and steel your hearts, but open up your ears, eyes, and most of all, your hearts to receive all that may be good in this land. I give you my assurance that there is a great deal of good in India." [9] (quoted from *Young India*, Aug. 6, 1925).

[9]Bharatiya Vidya Bhavan, Bombay, 1963.

World war starting in Europe did nothing to convince Gandhi of the importance of embracing Christianity: "The frightful outrage that is just going on in Europe perhaps shows that the message of Jesus of Nazareth, the Son of Peace, has been little understood in Europe and that light upon it may have been thrown from the East."[10] (quoted from *Speeches and Writings of M. Gandhi*, Feb.14, 1916)

Like Panikkar, Gandhi also mentioned the unfortunate alliance of imperialism and Christianity. He also resented proselytising under the cloak of humanitarian work in medicine and education. Finally he says:

"I have never been able to reconcile myself to the gaieties of the Christmas season. They have appeared to me to be so inconsistent with the life and teaching of Jesus.

"How I wish America could lead the way by devoting the season to a real moral stock-taking and emphasising consecration to the service of mankind for which Jesus lived and died on the cross."[11] (quoted from *Young India*, Dec.31, 1931)

Today missionaries are not permitted in some lands; in others they are not wanted by the people of other faiths; in a few countries some of the national Christians do not want them. One Christian political party in Pakistan demands the expulsion of missionaries and the nationalisation of Christian institutions. As Douglas Webster wrote: "The missionary calling is a permanent call to misunderstanding. It is important, however, to

[10]Ibid.,
[11]Ibid.,

learn from one's mistakes and to seek to remove misunderstandings and to benefit from criticisms."[12]

[12]*Yes to Mission*, p.26.

Do it yourself or do it with your friends:

1. Find some adverse criticism of the Christian faith in a newspaper or magazine.
2. Give a summary of the criticism.
3. Is it valid criticism?
4. What can Christians learn from it?

Chapter Thirteen

THE CASE FOR MISSIONS

The stage was set. There were three crosses and three prisoners. Three days after the execution one of them was alive again. Can you believe it?

Actually the Roman governor created the scene, but the Jewish religious leaders produced Act One. After the judge attempted to get him off, the innocent Galilean prisoner called Jesus the Nazarene was by false witness proved guilty and condemned to death. The Roman governor and judge, Pontius Pilate, washed his hands. Exit Pilate. Over to the army. The public who had clamoured for capital punishment came out to watch.

But what about the drama as a whole? There was a build-up. Rome constructed her roads — for her armies or for the couriers of Christ or for both? Peace throughout the empire — was it for trade or for quick communication of the most important of all messages?

Men were tired of their old religions and philosophies. They wanted something new and better. A minority of Jews were looking for a spiritual leader, not the romantic figure of a political deliverer.

Everyday Greek was the medium for trade bills and business letters throughout the empire — excellent for the memoirs of Tax Inspector Matthew, the case histories of Dr. Luke, and the correspondence of Paul of Tarsus.

Did this all just happen, or was it preparation? Was God producing the situation or was man? Right on time Christ died — not a few hours after the nailing but after all the centuries of preparation.

Death is the end. The religious and political authorities supported by the crowds had done their worst, and the three prisoners were dead. But, strange to relate, it was the prisoner in the middle who was really free. He, not the observers, was in charge of the situation. A dead man on a tree was master of ceremonies — not just then but forever afterwards.

He kept quiet for three days, and then right on time He walked out of His grave clothes and His tomb. One would not expect the Creator of time to be a second late. A final alarm clock is due to go off to end the world, and He will be here then too. He was born at a chosen time. He died at a time His Father appointed, and He will come back when His Father says so.

Is history man's story (his story) or God's story (His story)? Granted it is both, but God always has the first word and the last word and many in between.

We look at the chaos in the world. Civil war, violence, hijacking, kidnapping of ambassadors, the Middle East situation, Vietnam, Kashmir, and a dozen other trouble spots. Is God really in control? Is God using His church missions just on the periphery, or are they an integral part of the grand design?

Take China — communist for over a quarter of this century. Most missionaries left in 1951, the churches were persecuted, the circulation of the

Bible dropped. Every fourth person in the world is Chinese, so what is happening in China affects not only one quarter of the human race but the rest of us too. Over 800 million Chinese, half of whom are under 25, have now grown up under communism.

Take Brother Andrew's special feature article on China written in December 1968. He thinks God is in charge. Soon all roads will lead to China, just as they once all led to Rome. All those Chinese dialects? you say. No, basic Chinese now for 60 million copies of Mao's *Red Book*. Everyday Greek for the New Testament in Christ's day, and now basic Chinese.

Brother Andrew points out that the Chinese did not like listening. Too bad for the preacher, but the communists have forced their people to listen to communist indoctrination. We don't like force (that is man's work), but the communists may one day listen to God's words.

The past used to hold back even the Chinese Christian — customs, traditions, ancestors — but communism has smashed all this. Is it the final result, or is it a preparation?

Christians in Hong Kong are trying to build up a stock of one quarter million Bibles and one quarter million New Testaments in basic Chinese — rather few compared to the *Thoughts of Mao* (60 million copies). Some young people are in training now to become missionaries to China. Revolution or expansionist wars could change the whole picture overnight, and there would be an entrance for the Gospel in an unprecedented way.

A third of the world is communist, but it is still God's world. He is preparing for the Christian climax to history — the return of Jesus Christ and the judgment of the world. What you believe about mission and God's part in history affects what you do about it. That is why 15 eminent theologians drew up "The Frankfurt Declaration" at the sessions of their theological convention on 4 March, 1970. It has been translated into many languages and endorsed by many evangelicals.

Let us not swallow it whole, but let us examine it for ourselves. I am quoting the declaration below, not the introduction but the main body of it, the seven indispensable basic elements of mission. Discuss it point by point with your youth group or Christian fellowship.

The declaration leaves me with a query about the meaning of "humanisation" in section (ii) and a desire to delete the words in brackets in section (iii) about the ecumenical movement. I question the stress on baptism in sections (iv) and (vi) as I have known of several believers who never had the opportunity to be baptised.

Taken as a whole, it is a forthright clarification and statement in both positive and negative terms of the Biblical bases of mission. Judge for yourself.

THE FRANKFURT DECLARATION

(i) "Full authority in heaven and on earth has been committed to Me. Go forth therefore and make all nations My disciples; baptise men everywhere in the name of the Father and the Son and the Holy Spirit, and teach them to observe all that I have commanded you. And be assured, I am with you always, to the end of time." (Matthew 28:18-20)

We recognise and declare:

Christian mission discovers its foundation, goals, tasks, and the content of its proclamation solely in the commission of the resurrected Lord Jesus Christ, and His saving act as they are reported by the witness of the apostles and early Christianity in the New Testament. Mission is grounded in the nature of the Gospel.

We therefore oppose the current tendency to determine the nature and task of mission by socio-political analyses of our time and from the demands of the non-Christian world. We deny that what the Gospel has to say to people today at the deepest level is not evident before its encounter with them. Rather, according to the apostolic witness, the Gospel is normative and given once for all. The situation of encounter contributes only new aspects in the application of the Gospel. The surrender of the Bible as our primary frame of reference leads to the shapelessness of mission, and a confusion of the task of mission with a general idea of responsibility for the world.

(ii) "Thus will I prove myself great and holy and make Myself known to many nations; they shall know that I am the Lord" (Ezekial 38:23). "Therefore, Lord, I will praise Thee among the nations and sing psalms to Thy name." (Psalm 18:49 and Romans 15:9)

We recognise and declare:

The first and supreme goal of mission is the glorification of the name of the one God throughout the entire world and the proclamation of the Lordship of Jesus Christ, His Son.

We therefore oppose the assertion that mission today is no longer so concerned with the disclosure of God as with the manifestation of a new man and the extension of a new humanity into all social realms. Humanisation is not the primary goal of mission. It is rather a product of our new birth through God's saving activity in Christ within us, or an indirect result of the Christian proclamation in its power to perform a leavening activity in the course of world history.

A one-sided outreach of missionary interest toward man and his society leads to atheism.

(iii) "There is no salvation in anyone else at all, for there is no other name under heaven granted to men, by which we may receive salvation." (Acts 4:12)

We recognise and declare:

Jesus Christ our Saviour, true God and true man, as the Bible proclaims Him in His personal mystery and His saving work, is the basis, content, and authority of our mission. It is the goal of this mission to make known to all people in all walks of life the gift of His salvation.

We therefore challenge all non-Christians, who belong to God on the basis of creation, to believe in Him and to be baptised in His name, for in Him alone is eternal salvation promised to them.

We therefore oppose the false teaching (which is circulated in the ecumenical movement since the Third General Assembly of the World Council of Churches in New Delhi) that Christ Himself is anonymously so evident in world religions, historical changes, and revolutions that man can encounter Him and find salvation in Him without the direct news of the Gospel.

We likewise reject the unbiblical limitation of the person and work of Jesus to His humanity and ethical example. In such an idea the uniqueness of Christ and the Gospel is abandoned in favour of a humanitarian principle which others might also *find in other religions and ideologies.*

(iv) "God loved the world so much that He gave His only Son, that everyone who has faith in Him may not die but have eternal life" (John 3:16). "In Christ's name, we implore you, be reconciled to God!" (2 Corinthians 5:20)

We recognise and declare:

Mission is the witness and presentation of eternal salvation performed in the name of Jesus Christ by His church and fully authorised messengers by means of preaching, the sacraments, and service. This salvation is due to the sacrificial crucifixion of Jesus Christ which occurred once for all and for all mankind.

The appropriation of this salvation to individuals takes place first, however, through proclamation which calls for decision and through baptism which places the believer in the service of love. Just as belief leads through repentance and baptism to eternal life, so unbelief leads through its rejection of the offer of salvation to damnation.

We therefore oppose the universalistic idea that in the crucifixion and resurrection of Jesus Christ all men of all times are already born again and already have peace with Him, irrespective of their knowledge of the historical saving activity of God or belief in it. Through such a misconception the evangelising commission loses both its full, authoritative power and its urgency. Unconverted men are thereby lulled into a fateful sense of security about their eternal destiny.

(v) "But you are a chosen race, a royal priesthood a dedicated nation, and a people claimed by God for His own, to proclaim the triumphs of Him who

has called you out of darkness into His marvellous light" (1 Peter 2:9). "Adapt yourselves no longer to the pattern of this present world."(Romans 12:2)

We recognise and declare:

The primary visible task of mission is to call out the messianic, saved community from among all people.

Missionary proclamation should lead everywhere to the establishment of the church of Jesus Christ, which exhibits a new, defined reality as salt and light in its social environment.

Through the Gospel and the sacraments, the Holy Spirit gives the members of the congregation a new life and an eternal, spiritual fellowship with each other and with God, who is real and present with them. It is the task of the congregation through its witness to move the lost - especially those who live outside its community - to a saving membership in the body of Christ. Only by being this new kind of fellowship does the church present the Gospel convincingly.

We therefore oppose the view that the church, as the fellowship of Jesus, is simply a part of the world. The contrast between the church and the world is not merely a distinction in function and in knowledge of salvation; rather, it is an essential difference in nature. We deny that the church has no advantage over the world except the knowledge of the alleged future salvation of all men.

We further oppose the one-sided emphasis on salvation which stresses only this world, according to which the church and the world together share in a future, purely social reconciliation of all mankind. That would lead to the self-dissolution of the church.

*(vi) "Remember then your former condition ...
you were at that time separate from Christ, strang-
ers to the community of Israel, outside God's
covenants and the promise that goes with them.
Your world was a world without hope and without
God." (Ephesians 2:11,12)*

We recognise and declare:

*The offer of salvation in Christ is directed with-
out exception to all men who are not yet bound
to Him in conscious faith. The adherents to the
non-Christian religious and world views can receive
this salvation only through participation in faith.
They must let themselves be freed from their
former ties and false hopes in order to be admitted
by belief and baptism into the body of Christ.
Israel, too, will find salvation in turning to Jesus
Christ.*

*We therefore reject the false teaching that the
non-Christian religions and world views are also
ways of salvation similar to belief in Christ.*

*We refute the idea that "Christian presence"
among the adherents to the world religions and a
give-and-take dialogue with them are substitutes
for a proclamation of the Gospel which aims at
conversion. Such dialogues simply establish good
points of contact for missionary communication.*

*We also refute the claim that the borrowing of
Christian ideas, hopes and social procedures - even
if they are separated from their exclusive relation-
ship to the person of Jesus - can make the world
religions and ideologies substitutes for the church
of Jesus Christ. In reality they give them a syn-
cretistic and therefore anti-Christian direction.*

*(vii) "And this Gospel of the Kingdom will be
proclaimed throughout the earth as a testimony*

to all nations; and then the end will come."
(Matthew 24:14)

We recognise and declare:

The Christian world mission is the decisive, continuous saving activity of God among men between the time of the resurrection and second coming of Jesus Christ. Through the proclamation of the Gospel, new nations and people will progressively be called to decision for or against Christ.

When all people have heard the witness about Him and have given their answer to it, the conflict between the church of Jesus Christ and the world, led by the Antichrist, will reach its climax. Then Christ Himself will return and break into time, disarming the demonic power of Satan and establishing His own visible, boundless messianic kingdom.

We refute the unfounded idea that the eschatological expectation of the New Testament has been falsified by Christ's delay in returning and is therefore to be given up.

We refute at the same time the enthusiastic and utopian idealogy that either under the influence of the Gospel or by the anonymous working of Christ in history all of mankind is already moving toward a position of general peace and justice and will finally — before the return of Christ — be united under Him in a great world fellowship.

We refute the identification of messianic salvation with progress, development, and social change. The fatal consequence of this is that efforts to aid development and revolutionary involvement in the places of tension in society are seen as the contemporary forms of Christian mission. But such an identification would be a self-deliverance to the utopian movements of our time in the direction of their ultimate destination.

We do, however, affirm the determined advocacy of justice and peace by all churches, and we affirm that "assistance in developments" is a timely realisation of the divine demand for mercy and justice as well as the command of Jesus: "Love thy neighbour."

We see therein an important accompaniment and verification of mission. We also affirm the humanising results of conversion as signs of the coming messianic peace.

We stress, however, that unlike the eternally valid reconciliation with God through faith in the Gospel, all of our social achievements and partial successes in politics are bound by the eschatological "Not yet" of the coming kingdom, and the not yet annihilated power of sin, death, and the devil, who still is the "prince of this world."

This establishes the priorities of our missionary service and causes us to extend ourselves in the expectation of Him, who promises, "Behold! I make all things new." (Revelation 21:5, RSV)

(All Biblical quotations are from the New English Bible unless otherwise stated.)

Do it yourself or do it with your friends:

It Pays to Increase Your Word Power

1.Missiology is the study of: missiles; missions; missals.

2.Ecumenism is: a Biblical word; a movement for unity; a common denominator.

3.Syncretism is connected with: sin; a fusion of religions.

4.Comity is: "denominationalism by geography"; the opposite of enmity.

5.Intermission is: an interval; co-operation by missions.

6.Mahendra is: a place; a king; a religion.

7.Furlough is: a temporary transfer; a holiday; home leave.

8.Afghani is: an inhabitant of Afghanistan; a coin of Afghanistan.

9.Ethnocentric means: me first; my people first; my God first.

10.Deputation work is: work you give to others; reporting to others.

Answers below.

Answers to It Pays to Increase Your Word Power

1.Missiology is a study of missions.
2.Ecumenism is a movement for unity.
3.Syncretism is a fusion of religions.
4.Comity is "denominationalism by geography."
5.Intermission is co-operation between missions.
6.Mahendra is king of Nepal.
7.Furlough is home leave.
8.Afghani is a coin.
9.Ethnocentric means my people first.
10.Deputation work is reporting to others.

Chapter Fourteen

MOBILE AND FLEXIBLE

In the 1960s missionaries sailed; in the 1970s they fly; in the 1980s they may drive. The closure of the Suez Canal, making sea travel more expensive than air travel, the slump in the aeroplane industry in the 1970s, and the improvement of roads like the Asian Highway are all economic factors affecting mobility and methods of transport. People are determined to get around, even to the moon.

There are bamboo curtains, literal walls dividing cities like Berlin and Jerusalem, cold wars and economic sanctions, cease-fire lines which have held for a generation — all factors crippling understanding and real communication. But there are satellites aiding radio and TV, breakthroughs in mass media which mean we can have instant information and distilled facts about any country or tribe.

Clearly what is needed for the church in such a world is flexibility of policy and mobility of personnel. Flexibility without mobility is useless — it is knowing what to do but through paralysis being unable to do it. Mobility is really an attitude of mind — flexibility, if you like. Too many missions are hide-bound, fixed in ruts, traditional, more backward-looking than forward-thinking.

A blueprint for the 1970s won't do. Something

more daring is required - a commitment to the Father, Son and Holy Spirit which may lead into undreamed-of courses, policies, and plans; willingness to make plans, adapt them, or drop them.

Paul never saw a revolving door, but his alertness and responsiveness to the Holy Spirit would have enabled him to try doors and see if they opened and to try again if they didn't. China won't be closed forever, and India may not be open forever. Closed doors are NO reason for never looking that way again. You walk into a supermarket, and the doors open just as you get to them. If God guides you to enter a land now closed, why be too surprised, or disobedient?

Perhaps there should be a specifically Christian emergency force ready to take off to the trouble spots or disaster areas of the world to bring medical and economic relief along with the Red Cross and to share the love of Christ in words as well as deeds. Imagine a team of 20 from various nations, East as well as West, between them speaking many languages — adaptable, mobile, flexible. Supposing there is a call for economic, technical, and health development in a remote land, the Medical Assistance Programme and government-sponsored agencies may help, but it generally takes the churches two or three years to seize an opportunity. Why does it take communists less time? Because the churches have not learned the importance of flexibility and mobility.

Obviously there must be closer co-operation between missions, but that is not enough if the attitude of mind is rigid, not flexible. Roland Allen and Donald McGavran have argued for mobility in their respective decades and generations, but could the churches even now suddenly deploy even

20 extra workers to an area of Asia where God is manifestly at work? When missionaries had to leave China in 1951, it took several years for a redeployment. The demands of this decade require that expatriate church workers in one land be easily redeployed in another land if political pressures so demand.

Physically we live in the space age, in the jet age, but spiritually we think in terms of the early flights across the channel in the 1920s. Missions tend to be democratic rather than theocratic. Democracy is a polite term in our century, but it may belong to the first half of the century more than to the second half. Coup after coup occurs in Asia, and now it may be Africa's turn and South America's.

One-man-one-vote may be good for North America and Europe but it may not make for effective government. The average man may not have that flexibility of mind and adequate information with which to exercise his responsibilities.

I'm not arguing against democratic procedures but only pointing out that we cannot assume that the political procedures of the past may be adequate for emergencies, disasters, and crises which are now facing us.

In ecclesiastical matters the same may be true, and maybe this is why mission executives ask for more power to act (in consultation where possible). The average missionary has less to decide as the national churches assume their responsibilities and as co-operative ventures lay down their own policies. Matters affecting a mission working in several countries can more easily be decided by the "company" director, who is mobile enough to be really in touch with the international climate. His decisions should be based on first-hand contact with his missionary colleagues and national Christians.

There is a danger that missionary societies and fellowships may be run on dictatorial lines. This occurs when the idea of consultation is misused. Consultations should be recorded and endorsed by both or all sides. The documents are important — not so much the impression gained, which after all may be the wrong impression.

There is a tendency today to repudiate all that is past, to decry the "mission compound," the Christian complex, which rather isolates its employees and makes for a sort of ghetto. God guided in the past too, so we may not be required to sell off all these compounds and set off for the concrete jungles of the new cities. Jeremiah was ordered by God to buy land at a most unsuitable time; common sense advised against this purchase.

We agree that we face chaotic situations, so let us be unafraid to act when God gives the signal. Chaos can become order at His command. His service is perfect freedom — freedom not in spite of the past but because we are its heirs, and heirs of God and joint heirs with Christ. Let us enter our inheritance with a song and see in what exciting ways God will lead us through our wilderness.

Do it yourself or do it with your friends:

True or False

1. Many Protestant churches have closed in Eire.
2. Five percent of the population of France is communist or atheist.
3. The Gideons have placed 10,000 Bibles in hotels, prisons, ships, hospitals, and schools in Greece.
4. The population of Portugal is about nine million, but over 40 million Portuguese live in Brazil.
5. There are one million Muslims in Yugoslavia.
6. There are Korean missionaries in Thailand, Japanese missionaries in Laos, and Philippine missionaries in Indonesia.
7. Great Britain is the most literate nation on earth.
8. Tokyo with a population of over 10 million is the largest city in the world.

Answers below.

Answers to True or False

1. True.
2. False. Fifty percent of the population of France is communist or atheist.
3. True.
4. True.
5. False. There are over two million Muslims in Yugoslavia.
6. True.
7. False. Japan is the most literate nation in the world with 99% literacy.
8. True.

Chapter Fifteen

LET US PRAY

Is prayer a weak thing? God is in it, and the weakness of God is stronger than anything man-made. Man can only reach the moon, but prayer can reach God. Prayer can be a hot line to God about any situation in the world.

Many Christians think prayer is important but neglect it. The more one prays the more one believes in it. The less one prays the less one believes in it.

For prayer one needs a tranquil spirit. The rush hour on the tube is often preceded for the Christian by another rush hour which includes getting up, prayer, and breakfast. Ours is an age of rush, there is no rest for the wicked, and most of us are very wicked. Eternal motion rather than eternal peace is our experience. Reflection, meditation, contemplation belong to the monastery, not to the world.

What we really lack is discipline and self-denial. Even fasting is out of vogue. It is surprising how much time for prayer one has if one misses a few meals or even one or two regularly each week.

Arthur Wallis' *God's Chosen Fast* is a good book to read. Most of us have read enough books on the doctrine of prayer, but lack of time seems to hinder our practice. Arthur Wallis presents an answer. Some don't want answers.

Prayer for other lands is often mistakenly thought of as intercession. There are not many Christian Afghans to give thanks to God for Afghanistan. Should there be no thanksgiving for its mountains, its streams, its antiquity, its history, its poetry and music? Should there not be prayers of confession that for a thousand years the Christian church neglected that land? Request and intercession — yes, we are better at that because we understand quick returns.

What about praise? If the few Christians in Afghanistan — or for that matter in Oman or Saudi Arabia — neglect to praise the God and Father of our Lord Jesus Christ for who He is, no one else will do so.

Christ's prayer recorded in John's Gospel, chapter 17, was two-dimensional. It covered the world geographically, but it also concerned the future, "those who believe in Me through their word" (verse 20), and so it even reaches down to us. Most of our prayer is in one dimension, and we forget the generations yet to come. Perhaps there are not many yet to come, but if we are not around in the last days, others will be.

Sometimes prayer seems too easy. We would prefer hard work. Sometimes it seems too difficult, and we give up. We are not called to assess it but to engage in it. Christ prayed, and we are His disciples — or are we?

We have dealt with the matter of dropouts and casualties but not in relation to prayer. "In some cases missionaries are being sent abroad into strongly held enemy territory unarmed, unprotected, and largely untrained for spiritual warfare. No wonder there is such a high casualty rate, with so many returning disheartened, depressed, or ill.

"The situation at home is similar. Many Christian leaders and workers, who began their ministry full of hope and zeal, are now a shadow of the people they once were. They have been gradually worn down by hard and often fruitless work, not fully understanding the real nature of the battle nor how to win through against what often appear impossible odds. A modern general would be instantly dismissed if he dared to send such unprepared soldiers into battle against such a skillful and merciless enemy."[1]

We have underrated the enemy. Nuclear deterrents deal with nuclear weapons; firearms won't do. Prayer is the only weapon which defeats our enemy Satan.

"Satan is a past master at being indigenous. His work can look very respectable — on the surface. But behind the facade is immense power, vulnerable only to the authority of a Christian who believes in the power of the name of Jesus Christ."[2]

Muslim, Hindu, Buddhist prayer won't do. The hot line isn't hot if it isn't routed through Christ. Without Him we are out of touch with God. Through Him we are reconciled to God and kept in touch with God. Our sins cause occasional breakdowns. We have to admit the breakdown and call Him to put things right; then prayer is effective again.

Michael Harper speaks trenchantly on this point too: "The one who is free to move unmolested into enemy territory is the one who has a passion for righteousness and a hatred of evil, while a per-

[1]Michael Harper, *Spiritual Warfare* (Hodder and Stoughton, London, 1970), pp. 50-51.
[2]Ibid., p.59.

son who hankers after illicit pleasures, does Christian work for his own advantage, is undisciplined in his daily life, or is constantly self-indulgent will seldom be used to deliver others; on the contrary he may well be a stumbling-block to the other person's release and might well become a victim of the very thing from which he is trying to release the other person. St. Paul kept his body disciplined at all times, 'lest after preaching to others I myself should be disqualified' (1 Corinthians 9:27)." [3]

Communication and prayer are closely linked. We may be in touch with God but out of touch with the situation which we should bring to Him. One missionary secretary from a possibly praying church in England wrote to me: "I am most upset at the way the prayer request system is breaking up ....

"Is it because we, the church, do NOT pray? Is it because our prayers are ineffectual? That there is a blockage of sin or that we do not know or fail to observe the laws of prayer?

"Or is it that missionaries we support in prayer do not believe in it? Is it that they do not have the time to write, or is it lack of discipline? Is it that they do not see any results?

"Is it that prayer is not a practical thing? Is it time that we gave up asking for prayer requests each month? Certainly to try and give a picture of the needs of the mission field from an almost empty mail-bag is very difficult, and I wonder if it is not even deceitful to try."

To this the church has to give some answers, and the missionary too. The monthly sending of prayer requests by the missionary to the church

[3]Ibid., p.64.

seems a good system, especially if the missionary secretary of the church responsible for distributing the requests is able to read between the lines, remembering that missionaries often cannot write freely because of strong censorship.

The particular missionary secretary quoted writes the church news and prayer requests to the missionary, keeping him or her in touch with fashions in clothes, with trade union attitudes, current controversies and trends.

Another church I know never writes to its missionary, who sends regular prayer items and sometimes photos. Communication is a two-way affair. The New Testament, mainly a collection of letters, shows this.

Quite a number of people receive circular prayer letters from one or more missionaries but rarely, if ever, write back. One old lady I know always writes back. It is a good idea to receive one or two circulars regularly if one intends to pray regularly, and the move should come from the person at home.

Approach a missionary and get linked up. Find out about his society, his work, the country he works in. Take a deliberate and practical interest in another country apart from your own. This is part of going into all the world. If your church has taken on certain missionary responsibilities, these by virtue of your membership are also partly yours.

What is Jesus Christ doing now? He is praying. He is interceding for believers. If we follow Him, we follow Him in this. If we are joined to Him by faith, by faith we will share in His prayer ministry.

Do it yourself or do it with your friends:

1. Is it wrong not to pray for others? 1 Samuel 12:23.

2. Why should we pray for the Queen? 1 Timothy 2:1-4.

3. Why do we pray when we get in a tight spot? Nehemiah 1:4-5.

4. How much is prayer man-made? 1 Corinthians 14:15.

5. Should prayer be mainly intercession? Colossians 4:2.

6. What should we do about a labour shortage? Matthew 9:38.

7. Can we go it alone? Philippians 1:19.

8. Am I a spanner in the works? James 5:16.

9. When can I have a weekend off? Ephesians 6:10-12.

Chapter Sixteen

ME A MISSIONARY ?

The Missionary Fellowship to which I belong has a quarterly magazine called *GO*. Two other magazines also have this title; one relates to holidays. I have been wondering if this is a good title for our paper. Most of us do not go; we stay at home.

Who is a missionary? One who goes. A go-er, not a do-good-er. Someone who goes out or makes an exit — he is a missionary. He goes to an unknown situation, to an alien people, or to an unpredictable future, serving a "nonresidential" God. The miles covered do not matter so much as the barriers crossed.

Take Jesus. He pitched His tent in Palestine. His origin was foreign. He was never at home. He was different. He was on a mission.

Some people want to dispense with the word missionary and use international, but what of the South Indian doing missionary work in North India? Is he a national international? Some people say we are all missionaries. Yes, in one sense we are, just as we are all priests.

I admit I don't always own up to being a missionary. Sometimes I say I work with the church overseas, sometimes I say that I am in charge of a United Bible Training Centre. Sometimes I feel that my fellow traveller knows missionaries, and I tell him that I am one. Professionally I am a teacher, but by vocation I am a missionary. If you can find a better word, please let me know.

This chapter is really about you, not me. "Me a missionary?" That is the question before you, I have already answered it; I am a missionary. It is your question.

Many Christians avoid this question and so avoid answering it. They avoid it because they say they do not like the word missionary. They avoid it because they are afraid of what the answer may involve. They avoid it because they feel they are too well qualified or well endowed with talents to leave the rat race and get involved in an academic or technological backwater.

God who gave us talents has the right to use them as He wishes. Our Creator is the best judge of what we should do.

This brings us to another point. Some Christians simply do not consult God about overseas service. They consider themselves much needed at home but redundant abroad. The divine labour exchange might have other views. God might have employment for you somewhere else. Many consultations with God are needed to know His decision in this matter.

I am not suggesting that the answer to the question "Me a missionary?" should be yes. God's answer may be no. Unless you honestly grasp the question and seek God's answer, you will never know.

Do it yourself or do it with your friends:

Write a mission prayer for yourself.

KEY BOOKS

For Students:
Give Up Your Small Ambitions
  by Michael Griffiths,
  Inter-Varsity Press, London, 1970.

For church and mission leaders:
Missions in the Seventies
  by Dennis E. Clark,
  Scripture Union, London, 1970.

For all:
Customs, Culture, and Christianity
  by Eugene A. Nida,
  Tyndale Press, London, 1963.
God's Chosen Fast
  by Arthur Wallis,
  Victory Press, Eastbourne, Sussex, 1969.
God's Smuggler
  by Brother Andrew
  with John and Elizabeth Sherrill
  Hodder and Stoughton, London, 1968.
Missionary Opportunity Today,
  A brief world survey, edited by Leslie Lyall,
  Inter-Varsity Fellowship, London, 1963.
  (out of print)
Missions in Crisis
  by Eric S. Fife and Arthur F. Glasser,
  Inter-Varsity Press, London, 1961.
No Graven Image
  by Elisabeth Elliott,
  Harper & Row, New York, 1966.
  (out of print)

Spiritual Warfare
   by Michael Harper,
   Hodder and Stoughton, London, 1970.

A World to Win
   by Leslie Lyall
   Inter-Varsity Fellowship and Overseas Missionary Fellowship, London, 1972.

The World's Religions
   by Norman Anderson,
   Inter-Varsity Press, London, 1950.
   (out of print)

Yes to Mission
   by Douglas Webster,
   SCM Press, London, 1966.
   (out of print)

Addresses of Key Missions
UK Protestant Missions Handbook
   The Evangelical Missionary Alliance,
   19 Draycott Place, London SW3 2SJ

KEY BOOKLETS

"The Continuing Missionary Task"
   by Douglas Webster, Simon Booklets,
   Society for Promoting Christian Knowledge,
   London, 1962.

"Don't Soft-Pedal God's Call"
   by Michael Griffiths,
   Overseas Missionary Fellowship, London.

"The Missionary"
   by Theodore F. Romig and Archie R. Crouch,
   World Horizons, Inc., New York, 1965.

KEY MAGAZINES

Africa Challenge,
    published in West Africa through
    Sudan Interior Mission,
    84 Beulah Hill, Upper Norwood, London SE19.

East Asia Millions,
    monthly magazine of the Overseas Missionary
    Fellowship, Newington Green, London N16.

The International Review of Missions,
    2 Eaton Gate, Sloane Square, London SW1.

The Way,
    magazine of the International Fellowship of
    Evangelical Students, 27 Marylebone Road,
    London NW1.

Other recent paperbacks from Concordia:

FROM WITCHCRAFT TO CHRIST
by Doreen Irvine. 190 pages: paperback edition 60p, hardback edition: £1.50.

Doreen Irvine's remarkable story was written at the urging of her friends, of those who had been helped by her ministry, and of those who heard the testimony of how God brought her out of great evil, darkness, and doubt into His wonderful light. As "Daring Diana" she followed a life of prostitution, strip-tease, drink, drugs — eventually witchcraft, where she became Queen of Black Witches. When eventually freed from her sordid life and the power of demons, she became known as a trophy of grace.

70,000 copies sold in the first year of publication!

ECOLOGY CRISIS:
God's Creation and man's pollution
by John W. Klotz. 168 pages paperback edition 60p, hardback edition £1.50.

This is a most helpful introduction for the layman to the problems of our deteriorating environment. It contains an overview of the various types of pollution and asks the question "What is needed?" The author writes as a Christian and refers to the Biblical concept that man cannot claim to own anything.

FROM THE FOREST I CAME:
The Story of Gipsy Rodney Smith MBE
by David Lazell. 192 pages plus 8 pages photographs: paperback 40p, hardback £1.00.

Born on the outskirts of Epping Forest, Gipsy Rodney Smith MBE grew up to be one of the best-known personalities of his age, a friend of Statesmen and ordinary people alike. This biography relates how the young Gipsy lad grew up into a self-taught preacher, writer, singer, world-traveller and friend of millions. The profile of this unusually gifted man includes his love of nature, which was shared by his famous broadcasting nephew, "Romany of the B.B.C."

LEARNING TO USE YOUR BIBLE

by Oscar E. Feucht. 192 pages paperback edition 40p.

One reason for the inadequate and faulty use of the Scriptures (apart from the culture of our times) is the fact that few people have ever read a book which introduces the Bible to them, or taken a course which gives them the "keys" to the Biblical library. That is precisely the purpose of this publication. In a Foreword to this book, the Rev. A. Morgan Derham, Secretary for Information of the United Bible Societies, states: "It is important that Christians should have help in rightly understanding and applying the Scriptures. Any publication which serves this purpose is to be welcomed: 'Learning to Use your Bible' does it so well that it is more than welcome ...".